Understanding FRS 17

Retirement benefits

Understanding FRS 17

Retirement benefits

By Hans Nailor, FCA
of PricewaterhouseCoopers, Chartered Accountants
London, January 2001

Published by:

Gee Publishing Limited
100 Avenue Road
Swiss Cottage
London
NW3 3PG
Tel: +44 (020) 7393 7400
Fax:+44 (020) 7393 7463
Web site: www.gee.co.uk

This book aims to provide general guidance only and does not purport to deal with all the possible questions and issues that may arise in any given situation. Should the reader encounter particular problems he or she is advised to seek professional advice, which PricewaterhouseCoopers would be pleased to provide.

No responsibility for loss occasioned to any person acting or refraining from action as a result of any material in this publication can be accepted by the author or publisher.

FRS 17 is reproduced with the permission of the Accounting Standards Board Limited.

PricewaterhouseCoopers is authorised by the Institute of Chartered Accountants in England and Wales to carry on investment business.

ISBN 1860899323

Printed and bound in England by Ashford Colour Press Ltd

Preface

This book reproduces the text of Financial Reporting Standard No 17, 'Retirement benefits', and includes inserted within the paragraphs of the standard our interpretation, commentary and examples reproduced in colour. In addition, an executive summary of the main provisions of the standard is included at the front of the book, also reproduced in colour.

Acknowledgements

The author acknowledges with thanks the assistance given by Peter Holgate, Malcolm Woodford, Barry Johnson, Barbara Willis and Amber Rollinson in the preparation and production of this text.

January 2001

Contents

Contents

Appendices

Contents

Executive summary

Introduction

Accounting for pensions has been one of the most hotly debated topics in accounting. For many years accountants across the world have struggled to reach a consensus on how final salary pension schemes should be reflected in the employers' financial statements.

FRS 17, 'Retirement benefits', replaces SSAP 24, which has been the UK standard on pension costs since 1988, and introduces a completely different way for companies and other employers to account for those benefits. The changes principally affect employers that operate defined benefit schemes.

Before SSAP 24, the pension charge in a company's profit and loss account was normally based on the amount of cash contributions paid to the pension scheme during the financial year or, in the case of unfunded schemes, on the amount of pensions paid by the company. SSAP 24 introduced an accruals model, or 'income approach', for measuring the annual cost of providing pension benefits. The focus was on achieving a relatively stable charge in the profit and loss account, which broadly reflected an actuarial estimate of long-term contribution rates. Surpluses and deficits were accounted for by smoothing the pension costs over the service lives of the employees.

SSAP 24 had fallen into disrepute, however, largely because it produced balance sheet figures which were difficult, if not impossible, to understand. Another criticism of SSAP 24 was that the calculations were too much influenced by the assumptions made by actuaries when measuring pension obligations and scheme assets. Those measurement practices are now inconsistent with both IAS and US GAAP.

The new model in FRS 17 approaches pension cost accounting from a balance sheet perspective. It works from the premise that a surplus or deficit in a pension scheme (measured with reference to the fair values of the scheme assets and liabilities) should be shown on the employer's balance sheet. The overall figures in the performance statements reflect the

1

changes in those fair values year on year. For many companies this is expected to make a material difference to reported profits.

FRS 17 has a long implementation period. For the first two years only disclosures need to be given. The new figures do not need to be recognised in the financial statements until 2003. But companies will quickly need to understand the impact of the FRS so that compliance can be managed and the effect on key financial reporting measures (such as EBITDA), financing agreements and performance related compensation can be explained.

Field testing

PricewaterhouseCoopers carried out extensive research on the implications of FRS 17 during the development of the exposure draft, FRED 20. This research included restating the balance sheets, profit and loss accounts and statements of total recognised gains and losses (STRGL) for a number of companies and submitting the results to the Accounting Standards Board. Some of the key findings were:

- Pension costs will be more volatile. This is due to interest rate changes.

- Costs for current service will generally be higher than under SSAP 24. This is a direct consequence of a move to a market basis with current lower interest rates.

- Pension costs will be subjected to significant hikes when companies make benefit improvements. In general, these costs can no longer be spread or met out of surpluses.

- There are likely to be huge items in the STRGL, which in the field test in some years were as high as a third of net equity.

- Changing the discount rate by ½ per cent makes little difference to profit.

- The assumption for the expected return on assets makes a significant difference to pension costs.

Main features of FRS 17

Scope

FRS 17 applies to all types of benefits that an employer provides after employees have completed their service, including pensions and post-retirement healthcare benefits.

There is no SSAP 24-type exemption for overseas schemes that have been accounted for under a different accounting standard. All schemes should be accounted for consistently in compliance with the FRS and so adjustments will be required if necessary.

There are special arrangements for individual companies that participate in multi-employer pension schemes, including group schemes. In some circumstances the individual participating companies will treat the scheme as a defined contribution scheme.

Reflecting defined benefit schemes in the balance sheet

Pension scheme assets should be measured at fair value at each balance sheet date.

Pension scheme liabilities should be measured on an actuarial basis using the projected unit method. This considers promised benefits for pensioners and deferred pensioners and accrued benefits for members in service taking into account projected earnings. 'Best estimate' demographic and financial assumptions are required. The pension liabilities should be discounted at the current rate of return on a AA rated quality corporate bond of equivalent currency and term. The FRS requires a full actuarial valuation at least every three years. In-between an actuarial 'review' is required to ensure the valuation is updated for current conditions.

The net of these two figures gives the scheme surplus or deficit, which should be recognised as an asset or liability on the balance sheet. However, the asset or liability should be shown separately after all other assets and liabilities and net of attributable deferred tax. If a surplus is very large, the amount of the asset that is recognised on the balance sheet may need to be restricted to what the employer can recover *via* reduced future contributions or refunds.

Executive summary

The method of calculating the surplus or deficit will often lead to large variations in the 'pension balance' year on year. Market values of the scheme assets will fluctuate, as will the present value of the scheme liabilities, not least from applying different discount rates to the gross liability. But at least the pension balance will be a number that has some meaning for most readers and it will be clearly visible as a separate category on the face of the balance sheet.

Reporting performance

The use of market values in the balance sheet will often give rise to large and volatile changes in the amounts reported as pension assets or liabilities. The FRS identifies several components of performance and requires them to be reported as follows:

Profit and loss account		STRGL
Operating	**Financing**	
Current service cost (capital cost of benefits earned in current period)	Interest cost (interest on the accrued pension liabilities)	Differences between the actual and expected return on scheme assets
Past service costs (capital cost of benefit improvements)	Less: expected return on the assets held by the pension scheme	Experience changes affecting scheme liabilities
Gains and losses on curtailments and settlements (for example, early retirements, bulk transfers from scheme) – except where FRS 3 para 20 items		Effect of changes in actuarial assumptions

Under FRS 17, no credit (debit) is reflected in the operating costs for any surplus (deficit) in the scheme and so the cost is unrelated to whether, or how, the scheme is funded. This is a major change from SSAP 24, which required the operating pension cost to be reduced or increased by

4

spreading forward surpluses or deficits over the employees' remaining service lives.

FRS 17 moves the interest cost and expected return on scheme assets from the operating to the financing part of the profit and loss account. The interest cost is the notional interest cost arising from unwinding the discount on the scheme liabilities, based on the discount rate (that is, appropriate bond rate) at the beginning of the period. The expected return on assets is the actuarial forecast of total return (that is, income and gains) on the actual assets in the scheme. This is a long-term rate and is also set at the beginning of the period. The net cost or credit is affected by the funding of the scheme and may well be a credit as a result of a scheme being in surplus and/or a higher rate of return being applied to the scheme assets than the discount rate applied to the scheme liabilities.

The intention is that most of the volatility, which will be caused by changes in market values and assumptions, will be reflected in the STRGL. But the current service cost (an operating cost) is inherently variable too (unlike SSAP 24's regular cost) if, for example, the discount rate changes significantly year on year. Also the net cost or credit in the financing part of the profit and loss account could be variable as a result of, for example, changes in the rate of discount on the liability or in the expected rate of return on the scheme assets.

Disclosures

The disclosure requirements in respect of defined benefit schemes are substantial. They include:

- Main financial assumptions (individually) including inflation; rate of increase in salaries; increase for pensions in payment and deferred pensions; liability discount rate.

- Fair value of assets and expected rate of return for each class analysed between equities, bonds and other.

- Specified components of amounts included in operating profit, finance costs (or income) and the STRGL.

Executive summary

- Five year history of amounts recognised in the STRGL (showing the difference between expected and actual return on assets, the experience gains/losses on the scheme liabilities and the total actuarial gain or loss). This disclosure is not retrospective, however, and so the five-year record will not be complete until 2006.

- Analysis of the movements during the year in the surplus or deficit and, if applicable, a reconciliation of the surplus or deficit in the scheme to the asset or liability in the balance sheet.

If the employer has more than one scheme, combined disclosures may be given for appropriate groups of schemes.

Distributable profits

The defined benefit asset or liability will give rise to a gain or deficit in reserves. We believe there should be a working presumption that cumulative actuarial gains give rise to an unrealised profit and cumulative actuarial losses give rise to a realised loss, insofar as they are booked in the financial statements of an individual company. Hence the recognition of a defined benefit liability would reduce a company's distributable profits.

The possibilities of an unexpected impairment of distributable profits are mitigated, however, by FRS 17's rules relating to group defined benefit schemes. Where a scheme that covers more than one company does not enable the individual companies to identify their share of the scheme's assets and liabilities, the FRS requires each company (including the parent) to treat the scheme as a defined contribution scheme. Each individual company should, therefore, recognise only the contributions payable each year. The defined benefit accounting would be used, in these circumstances, only at the consolidation level. In these circumstances distributable profits are not impaired unless and until additional contributions become payable.

Groups that operate company-specific schemes may wish to consider restructuring their schemes to reduce the risk of sudden deficits appearing in individual companies' financial statements.

6

Main differences between FRS 17 and SSAP 24

A summary of the main differences between FRS 17 and SSAP 24 is set out below:

	FRS 17	SSAP 24
Valuation of scheme assets	Market values required	Asset values can be smoothed
Valuation of scheme liabilities	Projected unit method required	No single actuarial method specified
	Discount rate is AA bond yield	Discount rate typically reflects expected return on scheme assets
Actuarial gains and losses	Recognised immediately in STRGL	Spread forward in P&L over employees' remaining service lives
Balance sheet	Asset or liability is the difference between the value of scheme assets and value of scheme liabilities (net of deferred tax)	Asset or liability is the difference between the amounts recognised as cost and contributions paid
Balance sheet asset limitation	Recoverable surplus	No similar requirement (although Companies Act may prevent irrecoverable asset)

	FRS 17	SSAP 24
Benefit improvements that affect past service	Charged immediately to operating profit (but spread if benefits do not vest immediately)	Usually spread forward (cost of ex-gratia pensions can be met out of surplus)
Curtailments and settlements	Gains and losses recognised immediately in P&L	Complex rules – usually cash basis
Pension cost charge	Shown in three locations in P&L and STRGL	Shown as single figure in operating costs

Comparison with IAS 19

FRS 17 takes UK accounting for pension costs much closer to the international standard IAS 19 (revised), 'Employee benefits', but there are some important differences. A comparison of the main features is given below.

	FRS 17	IAS 19 (revised 1998)
Scope	Retirement benefits only	All employee benefits
Defined contribution schemes	Cost equals contributions payable	Comparable
Defined benefit schemes – assets	Market values at balance sheet date	Comparable
Defined benefit schemes – liabilities	Projected unit method required Discount rate is AA bond yield	Comparable

	FRS 17	**IAS 19 (revised 1998)**
Actuarial gains and losses	Recognised immediately in STRGL	Amortisation (to income statement) required if the cumulative unrecognised gains or losses at end of previous period exceed 10% of the greater of the value of the pension liabilities and plan assets (the 'corridor'). Excess is amortised over average remaining working lives of participating employees
		Permitted, however, is any systematic method that results in faster recognition provided that same method is applied consistently to gains and losses and period to period (for example, immediate recognition of all gains and losses, both within and outside the 'corridor' is permitted)

	FRS 17	**IAS 19 (revised 1998)**
Balance sheet	Asset or liability is the difference between the value of scheme assets and value of scheme liabilities (net of deferred tax)	Asset or liability does not reflect the surplus or deficit in the scheme (where actuarial gains and losses are not yet recognised), and is not net of deferred tax
	Asset amounts limited to recoverable surplus	Similar recoverability test
Benefit improvements that relate to past service	Charged immediately to operating profit (but spread if benefits do not vest immediately)	Comparable
Curtailments and settlements	Gains and losses recognised immediately in P&L	Comparable
Pension cost charge	Shown in three locations in P&L and STRGL	Components of cost are comparable, but actuarial gains and losses (to the extent recognised) are also shown in the income statement
	Interest cost and expected return on assets are shown as a net financial item adjacent to interest	IAS 19 does not specify whether interest cost and expected return on plan assets should be presented as operating or financial items

The most important difference between the two standards is that IAS 19 permits a mechanism for spreading actuarial gains and losses – the so-called 'corridor' approach (based on the US standard FAS 87). The ASB does not believe this approach has any conceptual merit. Its only function seems to be to protect the income statement from too much volatility. The ASB will be hoping to persuade the IASC to adopt the FRS 17 approach during the long transitional period. If it is unable to do so, we may see more changes to UK GAAP on pensions.

FRS 17's transitional arrangements

FRS 17 has unusual transitional arrangements. Although, as always, earlier adoption is encouraged, the FRS allows companies to continue to use the SSAP 24 rules until years ending before June 2003 (that is, until calendar 2002 for December year-ends). For companies that defer implementing FRS 17 until it becomes mandatory, progressive footnote disclosures are required for 2001 and 2002 in addition to the normal SSAP 24 disclosures:

- Years ending from June 2001 to May 2002 – disclosures relating to closing balance sheet amounts that would be recognised under the accounting requirements of the FRS.

- Years ending from June 2002 to May 2003 – disclosures relating to opening and closing balance sheet amounts, together with profit and loss and STRGL amounts (without comparatives) that would be recognised under the accounting requirements of the FRS.

If advantage is taken of the transitional arrangements, all the required comparatives will be available from the previous years' disclosures when the FRS has to be implemented in full. The required disclosures are illustrated in the body of this guide.

Early adoption

Final dates for implementation are:

- June 2001 for disclosures.

- June 2003 for full accounting.

Executive summary

There are a number of possible approaches to early adoption, for example:

- At any time between December 2000 and May 2001, give the FRS 17 transitional disclosures, but retain SSAP 24 accounting.

- At any time between December 2000 and May 2003, adopt FRS 17 accounting and disclosures in full.

- At any time between December 2000 and May 2003, give the full FRS 17 disclosures (that is, relating to the balance sheet and performance statements with comparatives), but retain SSAP 24 accounting.

Issues to consider for early adoption

The main reason for early adoption would be that the business takes a leadership position in its marketplace. This may be beneficial if the impact on earnings or other financial performance measures is positive compared to the competition. It may also be seen as a positive move if the pension scheme represents a major financial risk. This does rely on the right investor communication.

The are several issues to consider in deciding on the adoption date:

- During the transitional period, there is a possibility that the IASC will adopt FRS 17's approach of immediate recognition of actuarial gains and losses. As the EU intends to require listed companies to report under IAS by 2005, there is the risk that, if this does not work as the ASB hope, there will have to be another change to FRS 17. Some would, therefore, prefer to wait and see how the debate at international level develops before adopting FRS 17.

- A benefit of the transitional period is that actuaries can start doing valuations on the new FRS 17 basis without restating the past. Early adopters would have to restate their comparatives, which requires objective assessment of measures such as the expected return on assets in the previous year.

- Complying with FRS 17 for the first time requires education of subsidiary finance departments regarding the new reporting

12

requirements. There will be particular issues regarding information from overseas subsidiaries, where the present rules allow the use of foreign GAAP numbers without adjustment. This is no longer the case under FRS 17.

■ Meeting the company's financial reporting timetable requires careful planning, especially as regards the need for pension scheme asset and liability valuations in time for company rather than pension scheme reporting timetables.

■ Listed companies will need to consider implementing any year end change of policy in the interim accounts.

■ The actuarial profession, in conjunction with the auditing profession, is still developing guidance on a number of implementation issues such as the scope of the actuary's annual valuation in the context of companies' reporting timetables.

■ Some restructuring may be required to manage the effect of the balance sheet and P&L changes on finance agreements, for example covenants, (though 'frozen GAAP' may apply), performance-related compensation and distributable profits.

■ If benefit improvements are being considered in relation to a surplus, employers may wish to implement them before adopting FRS 17 in order to avoid the charge against operating profit.

■ The accounting measurements of surplus or deficit are likely to divorce the accounting valuations further from funding valuations. If a scheme is in surplus, consider whether the directors and the trustees will see eye to eye on the amount carried on the employer's balance sheet. Consider also the relationship with the Minimum Funding Requirement (MFR).

Types of pension scheme

Accounting for the cost of providing pension benefits is particularly affected by the type of benefits that are promised by a scheme and by the way in which the employer's obligations in respect of such benefits are funded. The broad classifications used in pensions terminology are

13

summarised below. Each involves a cost to the employer insofar as it is obligated to contribute towards the cost of the benefits receivable by its employees or their dependants.

Defined contribution schemes

Defined contribution schemes (often referred to as money purchase schemes) are pension schemes where the benefits are determined directly by the value of contributions paid in respect of each member and the investment performance achieved on those contributions. Normally, the rate of contribution to be paid by the employer company will be specified in the scheme's rules. If the investments have performed well the individual will obtain a higher pension than if the investments have performed badly. In such schemes the risk of poor investment performance lies with the individual.

Defined benefit schemes

Defined benefit schemes are pension schemes where the rules specify the benefits to be paid, typically by reference to final salary levels, and such schemes are financed accordingly. The majority of such schemes define benefits in relation to an employee's final salary (typically the pension will be based on 1/60th of final salary for each year of pensionable service, up to a maximum of 40 years). In the UK, they are often referred to as final salary schemes. Another, less common, form of defined benefit scheme is the average salary scheme where the pension is calculated by reference to average pay over an extended period. In defined benefit schemes the risk of poor investment performance lies with the sponsoring company.

Funded schemes

Funded pension schemes are schemes where the future liabilities for pension benefits are provided for in advance by the accumulation of assets held externally to the employing company's business. The assets are usually placed under the control of trustees, who administer the scheme in accordance with the provisions of trust law and the terms of the trust deed governing the particular scheme. Employer and employee contributions paid to the trust are invested by the trustees; pensions are paid out of the accumulated funds of the trust.

Most funded schemes in the UK that are established under trusts enjoy considerable tax benefits through Inland Revenue recognition as exempt approved schemes. The main benefits are:

■ Relief, as an expense, for the employer's contributions.

■ Relief for employees from assessment to tax both as regards employer's contributions and employees' own contributions.

■ Exemption from income or capital gains tax on investments held by the scheme, although the abolition of Advance Corporation Tax in 1997 means that tax approved pension schemes can no longer reclaim any tax associated with dividends from UK equities.

The Finance Act 1989 introduced an upper limit on the amount of salary that may be taken into account for pension purposes (the 'earnings cap'), which for the tax year 2000-2001 is £91,800. Since the Finance Act 1989, employers have been able to establish unapproved schemes to run alongside existing exempt approved schemes. Unapproved schemes can provide unlimited benefits and are mainly used to provide 'top-up' pensions for higher paid employees whose pensionable earnings in the exempt approved scheme are capped. Unapproved arrangements, which may be funded or unfunded, do not enjoy the tax benefits that apply to exempt approved schemes.

Unfunded schemes

Unfunded pension schemes are schemes where pension benefits are paid directly by the employer. No assets are set aside in advance to provide for future liabilities; instead pension liabilities are met out of the employer's own resources. Such schemes are not common in the private sector in the UK, but are the normal method of pension provision in Germany. They are also found in the public sector. However, the incidence of unfunded arrangements in the UK has increased, particularly in respect of higher paid executives as a result of changes in the Finance Act 1989 relating to the capping of pensions that affect approved funded schemes.

Personal pension and stakeholder schemes

Personal pension and stakeholder schemes are pension arrangements available to the self-employed, employees with no company scheme, employees with non-pensionable earnings and those who wish to contract out of the State Earnings Related Pension Scheme or opt out of an occupational pension scheme. These are defined contribution schemes.

Summary

a Financial Reporting Standard 17 sets out the requirements for accounting for retirement benefits.

Defined contribution schemes

b The cost of a defined contribution scheme is equal to the contributions payable to the scheme for the period.

Measurement of defined benefit scheme assets and liabilities

c Defined benefit scheme assets are measured at fair value.

d Defined benefit scheme liabilities are measured using the projected unit method.

e Defined benefit scheme liabilities are discounted at the current rate of return on a high quality corporate bond of equivalent term and currency to the liability.

f Full actuarial valuations should be obtained at intervals not exceeding three years and should be updated at each balance sheet date.

Recognition of defined benefit schemes

g An asset is recognised to the extent that an employer can recover a surplus in a defined benefit scheme through reduced contributions and refunds. A liability is recognised to the extent that the deficit reflects the employer's legal or constructive obligation.

h The resulting defined benefit asset or liability is presented separately on the face of the balance sheet after other net assets.

i   The change in the defined benefit asset or liability (other than that arising from contributions to the scheme) is analysed into the following components:

     (i)   the current service cost

     (ii) the interest cost

     (iii) the expected return on assets

     (iv) actuarial gains and losses

     (v) past service costs (if any)

     (vi) settlements and curtailments (if any).

j   The current service cost and interest cost are based on the discount rate at the beginning of the period. The expected return on assets is based on the expected rate of return at the beginning of the period. The current service cost is shown within the appropriate statutory heading for pension costs in the profit and loss account. The interest cost and expected return on assets are shown as a net amount of other finance costs (or income) adjacent to interest.

k   The expected return is calculated by applying the expected rate of return over the long term to the market value of scheme assets at the beginning of the year, adjusted for any contributions received and benefits paid during the year. Although the expected rate of return will vary according to market conditions it is expected that the amount of the return will normally be relatively stable.

l   Actuarial gains and losses are recognised immediately in the statement of total recognised gains and losses. They are not recycled into the profit and loss account in subsequent periods.

m   Past service costs are recognised in the profit and loss account over the period until the benefits vest. If the benefits vest immediately, the past service cost is recognised immediately.

n   Gains and losses arising on settlements and curtailments are recognised immediately in the profit and loss account.

Disclosures for defined benefit schemes

o   The following disclosures are required:

(i)   the main assumptions underlying the scheme

(ii)   an analysis of the assets in the scheme into broad classes and the expected rate of return on each class

(iii) an analysis of the amounts included (a) within operating profit, (b) within other finance costs and (c) within the statement of total recognised gains and losses

(iv)   a five-year history of (a) the difference between the expected and actual return on assets, (b) experience gains and losses arising on the scheme liabilities and (c) the total actuarial gain or loss

(v)   an analysis of the movement in the surplus or deficit in the scheme over the period and a reconciliation of the surplus/deficit to the balance sheet asset/liability.

Financial Reporting Standard 17

Objective

1   The objective of this FRS is to ensure that:

   (a) financial statements reflect at fair value the assets and liabilities arising from an employer's retirement benefit obligations and any related funding;

   (b) the operating costs of providing retirement benefits to employees are recognised in the accounting period(s) in which the benefits are earned by the employees, and the related finance costs and any other changes in value of the assets and liabilities are recognised in the accounting periods in which they arise; and

   (c) the financial statements contain adequate disclosure of the cost of providing retirement benefits and the related gains, losses, assets and liabilities.

Definitions

2   The following definitions shall apply in the FRS and in particular in the Statement of Standard Accounting Practice set out **in bold type**.

Actuarial gains and losses:-

Changes in actuarial deficits or surpluses that arise because:

   (a) events have not coincided with the actuarial assumptions made for the last valuation (experience gains and losses) or

(b) the actuarial assumptions have changed.

Current service cost:-

The increase in the present value of the scheme liabilities expected to arise from employee service in the current period.

Curtailment:-

An event that reduces the expected years of future service of present employees or reduces for a number of employees the accrual of defined benefits for some or all of their future service. Curtailments include:

(a) termination of employees' services earlier than expected, for example as a result of closing a factory or discontinuing a segment of a business, and

(b) termination of, or amendment to the terms of, a defined benefit scheme so that some or all future service by current employees will no longer qualify for benefits or will qualify only for reduced benefits.

Defined benefit scheme:-

A pension or other retirement benefit scheme other than a defined contribution scheme.

Usually, the scheme rules define the benefits independently of the contributions payable, and the benefits are not directly related to the investments of the scheme. The scheme may be funded or unfunded.

Defined contribution scheme:-

A pension or other retirement benefit scheme into which an employer pays regular contributions fixed as an amount or as a percentage of pay and will have no legal or constructive obligation to pay further contributions if the scheme does not have sufficient assets to pay all employee benefits relating to employee service in the current and prior periods.

An individual member's benefits are determined by reference to contributions paid into the scheme in respect of that member, usually increased by an amount based on the investment return on those contributions.

Defined contribution schemes may also provide death-in-service benefits. For the purposes of this definition, death-in-service benefits are not deemed to relate to employee service in the current and prior periods.

Expected rate of return on assets:-

The average rate of return, including both income and changes in fair value but net of scheme expenses, expected over the remaining life of the related obligation on the actual assets held by the scheme.

Interest cost:-

The expected increase during the period in the present value of the scheme liabilities because the benefits are one period closer to settlement.

Past service cost:-

The increase in the present value of the scheme liabilities related to employee service in prior periods arising in the current period as a result of the introduction of, or improvement to, retirement benefits.

Projected unit method:-

An accrued benefits valuation method in which the scheme liabilities make allowance for projected earnings. An accrued benefits valuation method is a valuation method in which the scheme liabilities at the valuation date relate to:

(a) the benefits for pensioners and deferred pensioners (ie individuals who have ceased to be active members but are entitled to benefits payable at a later date) and their dependants, allowing where appropriate for future increases, and

(b) the accrued benefits for members in service on the valuation date.

The accrued benefits are the benefits for service up to a given point in time, whether vested rights or not.

Guidance on the projected unit method is given in the Guidance Note GN26 issued by the Faculty and Institute of Actuaries.

Retirement benefits:-

All forms of consideration given by an employer in exchange for services rendered by employees that are payable after the completion of employment.

Retirement benefits do not include termination benefits payable as a result of either (i) an employer's decision to terminate an employee's employment before the normal retirement date or (ii) an employee's decision to accept voluntary redundancy in exchange for those benefits, because these are not given in exchange for services rendered by employees.

Scheme liabilities:-

The liabilities of a defined benefit scheme for outgoings due after the valuation date.

Scheme liabilities measured using the projected unit method reflect the benefits that the employer is committed to provide for service up to the valuation date.

Settlement:-

An irrevocable action that relieves the employer (or the defined benefit scheme) of the primary responsibility for a pension obligation and eliminates significant risks relating to the obligation and the assets used to effect the settlement. Settlements include:

(a) a lump-sum cash payment to scheme members in exchange for their rights to receive specified pension benefits;

(b) the purchase of an irrevocable annuity contract sufficient to cover vested benefits; and

(c) the transfer of scheme assets and liabilities relating to a group of employees leaving the scheme.

Vested rights:-

These are:

(a) for active members, benefits to which they would unconditionally be entitled on leaving the scheme;

(b) for deferred pensioners, their preserved benefits;

(c) for pensioners, pensions to which they are entitled.

Vested rights include where appropriate the related benefits for spouses or other dependants.

Scope

3 **The FRS applies to all financial statements that are intended to give a true and fair view of a reporting employer's financial position and profit or loss (or income and expenditure) for a period.**

4   The FRS covers all retirement benefits that an employer is committed to providing, whether the commitment is statutory, contractual or implicit in the employer's actions. It applies to retirement benefits arising overseas, as well as those arising in the UK and the Republic of Ireland. Retirement benefits include, for example, pensions and medical care during retirement.

4.1   Unlike SSAP 24, there is no concession to multinational groups in respect of overseas schemes that have been accounted for under a different accounting standard. SSAP 24 encouraged the pension costs relating to overseas schemes to be adjusted to conform with SSAP 24, but did not require this if it was considered impracticable and costly to obtain the necessary actuarial information. All schemes should be accounted for consistently in compliance with the FRS and so adjustments will be required, where necessary, to convert retirement benefits accounting from local GAAP to a measurement and recognition basis that complies with the FRS.

4.2   The FRS also includes within its scope other post-retirement benefits that hitherto have been dealt with by UITF Abstract 6. UITF 6 addressed principally the accounting for post-retirement private medical insurance benefits, which are commonly provided in the US by UK groups with US subsidiaries. For those US operations that are governed by the requirements of the equivalent US standard FAS 106, UITF 6 permitted the FAS 106 numbers to be used in the UK accounts. When the FRS is adopted in full, that option is withdrawn.

5   The FRS covers funded and unfunded retirement benefits, including schemes that are operated on a pay-as-you-go basis, whereby benefits are paid by the employer in the period they fall due and no payments are made to fund benefits earned in the period. The FRS requires a liability to be recognised as the benefits are earned, not when they are due to be paid. The fact that the employer is funded by central government (or any other body) is not a reason for the employer not to recognise its own liabilities arising under the FRS.

6   **Reporting entities applying the Financial Reporting Standard for Smaller Entities currently applicable are exempt from the FRS.**

Defined contribution schemes

7   **The cost of a defined contribution scheme is equal to the contributions payable to the scheme for the accounting period. The cost should be recognised within operating profit in the profit and loss account.**

Multi-employer schemes

8   Where more than one employer participates in a defined contribution scheme, no special problems arise, since the employer's cost is limited to the contributions payable.

9   **Where more than one employer participates in a defined benefit scheme the employer should account for the scheme as a defined benefit scheme unless:**

   (a) the employer's contributions are set in relation to the current service period only (ie are not affected by any surplus or deficit in the scheme relating to past service of its own employees or any other members of the scheme). If this is the case, the employer should account for the contributions to the scheme as if it were a defined contribution scheme.

   (b) the employer's contributions are affected by a surplus or deficit in the scheme but the employer is unable to identify its share of the underlying assets and liabilities in the scheme on a consistent and reasonable basis. If this is the case, the employer should account for the contributions to the scheme as if it were a defined contribution scheme but, in addition, disclose:

   (i)   the fact that the scheme is a defined benefit scheme but that the employer is unable to identify its share of the underlying assets and liabilities; and

   (ii) any available information about the existence of the surplus or deficit in the scheme and the implications of that surplus or deficit for the employer.

10   Most multi-employer schemes will set contributions from employers so as to make good any deficit in the scheme and may reduce contributions to enable employers to benefit from a surplus. However, in some multi-employer schemes, an employer may have no obligation other than to pay a contribution that reflects only the benefits earned in the current period. In this case, from the point of view of the employer, the scheme is a defined contribution scheme and is accounted for as such. For this to be the case, there must be clear evidence that the employer cannot be required to pay additional contributions to the scheme relating to past service, including the existence of a third party that accepts that it has an obligation to fund the pension payments should the scheme have insufficient assets.

10.1   Such schemes are likely to be very rare – possibly non-existent – in the private sector.

11   An employer may be required to make contributions set at a level to make good any deficit but may be unable to identify its share of the underlying assets and liabilities in the scheme on a consistent and reasonable basis. This may be the case if the scheme exposes the participating employers to actuarial risks associated with the current and former employees of other entities, for example when the contributions from employers are set at a common level rather than reflecting the characteristics of the workforces of individual employers.

11.1   Some employers participate in industry-wide pension schemes, which provide centralised pension arrangements for identifiable groups of unrelated employers. Examples in the UK include the merchant navy pension funds for seafaring employees, the Electricity Supply Pension Scheme and schemes in the coal industry. Where the arrangements are of the defined benefit type, each employer should follow the defined benefit accounting rules of FRS 17 if the assets and accrued pension liabilities in the scheme can be allocated to individual participating employers. Each employer would recognise an asset or liability relating to its share

28

of the scheme assets less liabilities, and measure components of pension cost in the same manner as an entity that operates its own scheme. In other cases, each employer should treat the scheme as a defined contribution scheme, where the accounting is determined by the contributions payable for each period – no surplus or deficit, or actuarial gain or loss is recognised.

12   Subsidiaries are not exempt from the FRS and, where possible, will account for defined benefit schemes in accordance with its requirements. However, many group schemes are run on a basis that does not enable individual companies within the group to identify their share of the underlying assets and liabilities. In these circumstances, the individual companies (including the parent company) within the group will account for the scheme as a defined contribution scheme and will give the additional disclosures required above. From the point of view of the group entity, a group defined benefit scheme is not a multi-employer scheme and is treated as any other defined benefit scheme.

12.1 Group schemes often apply common contribution rates across the group as a whole. Also groups may undergo reorganisations of their company structures, and disposals and acquisitions occur. In such situations it may be impracticable to allocate pension scheme assets and liabilities to individual participating companies. As an example, a group scheme may have past service liabilities for pensioners or deferred pensioners of former subsidiaries that are no longer in the group. Paragraph 12 clarifies that the parent company in a group scheme is not excluded from the defined contribution treatment where the condition in paragraph 9 is met. Therefore, in many group schemes all of the participating companies will show pension costs equal to the contributions payable for the period. The defined benefit accounting rules would be used only at the consolidation level. A consolidation adjustment will be required to replace the total of the pension costs in the companies' financial statements (based on contributions payable) with the specified components of pension cost for a defined benefit scheme. In addition, any surplus or deficit in the group scheme will be recognised as an asset or liability in the consolidated balance sheet only. In those circumstances the figures in the consolidated financial statements will not be the same as the total of the figures shown in the individual group companies' financial statements. But, as required by paragraph 9(b), the individual company financial statements should disclose that the scheme is a defined benefit scheme, explain why defined benefit accounting is not used and disclose any available information about a surplus or deficit in the group scheme and the implications for that company – for example, the effect on future contribution rates. Where defined contribution accounting is adopted by individual companies, this has an important bearing on distributable profits (see commentary on paragraph 90).

Measurement of defined benefit schemes

13   Paragraphs 14-36 of the FRS set out the requirements for measuring the assets and liabilities within a defined benefit scheme (the scheme assets and the scheme liabilities). The recognition of an asset or liability and the movements therein in the financial statements of the employer arising from the defined benefit scheme measured on this basis is covered in paragraphs 37-74.

Scheme assets

14   Assets in a defined benefit scheme should be measured at their fair value at the balance sheet date.

15   Scheme assets include current assets as well as investments. Any liabilities such as accrued expenses should be deducted.

16   For quoted securities, the mid-market value is taken as the fair value. For unquoted securities, an estimate of fair value is used. The fair value of unitised securities is taken to be the average of the bid and offer prices.

17   Property should be valued at open market value or on another appropriate basis of valuation determined in accordance with the Appraisal and Valuation Manual published by the Royal Institution of Chartered Surveyors and the Practice Statements contained therein.

17.1 The SORP 'The Financial Reports of Pension Schemes' gives some guidance on property valuation from the perspective of pension fund trustees (the SORP also requires properties held by pension schemes to be included at market value at each balance sheet date). It notes the following circumstances in which open market value may not be the appropriate basis of valuation (the same guidance was included in FRED 20, but has not been retained in the FRS):

■ Properties in the occupation of the pension scheme, which should be valued on the basis of the existing use value.

■ Properties held fully equipped as operational entities, which should be valued having regard to trading potential.

■ Properties under construction or in the course of development or redevelopment, reconstruction or refurbishment which, depending upon the circumstances, including the stage of construction reached, should be valued either on the basis of open market value of the land and buildings in their existing state or on the basis of open market value of the land plus the cost of development incurred.

17.2 SSAP 19, FRS 15 and the pension scheme SORP all have requirements for properties to be measured at their open market value. None of those statements requires all properties to be fully revalued each year by external valuers, but each sets out guidelines for ensuring valuations are kept up to date in the financial statements. That guidance should be useful for establishing reliable valuation policies for the purpose of this FRS. For example, the SORP recommends that where property comprises a significant proportion of total investments, valuations should be carried out by independent valuers at least at the same frequency as actuarial valuations of the fund (normally every three years). It recommends that in other cases, properties may be included on the basis either of an annual valuation by an internal or external valuer or, where the proportion of property assets within total investments justifies a less frequent valuation, on a rolling basis over three or five years by an internal or external valuer, with an independent valuation of the entire property portfolio at least every five years. The SORP notes that more frequent valuations may be necessary in the case of properties in the course of development, redevelopment or refurbishment where there is a risk of cost overrun.

18   Insurance policies that exactly match the amount and timing of some or all of the benefits payable under the scheme should be measured at the same amount as the related obligations. For other insurance policies there are a number of possible valuation methods. A method should be chosen which gives the best approximation to fair value given the circumstances of the scheme.

19   Notional funding of a pension scheme does not give rise to assets in a scheme for the purposes of the FRS.

19.1 The FRS does not provide a definition of 'scheme assets'. Identifying scheme assets is important because the accounting for them is quite different from the accounting for other investments that are not scheme assets. This applies to both the balance sheet and the performance statements. In the balance sheet, scheme assets less scheme liabilities are shown as a net item. In the performance statements, the profit and loss account is credited each period with the expected long-term rate of return (income plus capital growth) on the scheme assets; differences between the expected and actual return are recognised as actuarial gains or losses in the STRGL.

19.2 There are several references in the FRS to scheme assets being assets *held* by the scheme. Furthermore, the ASB's rationale for the 'net' treatment of scheme assets and liabilities (paragraph 25 of Appendix IV) is that such assets are held in trust and are controlled by the scheme trustees rather than the employer. In the UK, scheme assets should usually be apparent from the way funded pension schemes are constituted. The assets are usually placed under the control of trustees, who administer the scheme in accordance with the provisions of trust law and the terms of the trust deed governing the particular scheme.

19.3   In some other countries, the identification of scheme assets may not be so clear cut. IAS 19 provides the following definition (revised in November 2000), which is useful guidance for UK groups with overseas schemes:

"Assets held by a long-term employee benefit fund are assets (other than non-transferable financial instruments issued by the reporting enterprise) that:

(a)   are held by an entity (a fund) that is legally separate from the reporting enterprise and exists solely to pay or fund employee benefits; and

(b)   are available to be used only to pay or fund employee benefits, are not available to the reporting enterprise's own creditors (even in bankruptcy), and cannot be returned to the reporting enterprise, unless either:

(i)   the remaining assets of the fund are sufficient to meet all the related employee benefit obligations of the plan or the reporting enterprise; or

(ii)   the assets are returned to the reporting enterprise to reimburse it for employee benefits already paid."

Scheme liabilities

Actuarial method and assumptions

20   Defined benefit scheme liabilities should be measured on an actuarial basis using the projected unit method. The scheme liabilities comprise:

> **(a) any benefits promised under the formal terms of the scheme; and**
>
> **(b) any constructive obligations for further benefits where a public statement or past practice by the employer has created a valid expectation in the employees that such benefits will be granted.**

21   Where the scheme rules require a surplus arising in the scheme to be shared between the employer and members (perhaps in conjunction with a similar sharing of deficits), or where past practice has established a valid expectation that this will be done, the amount that will be passed to members should be treated as increasing the scheme liabilities.

21.1   The components of scheme liabilities specified in paragraph 20 reflect the characteristics of a 'present obligation' in FRS 12. The recognition of a provision stems from the existence of a present obligation. A present obligation may be legal or constructive. A constructive obligation may be more difficult to discern in practice than a legal obligation as it derives from the employer's actions. FRS 12 defines a constructive obligation as:

"An obligation that derives from an entity's actions where:

(a) by an established pattern of past practice, published policies or a sufficiently specific current statement, the entity has indicated to other parties that it will accept certain responsibilities; and

(b) as a result, the entity has created a valid expectation on the part of those other parties that it will discharge those responsibilities."

21.2   An example of a constructive obligation is a practice of granting annual increases to pensions in payment and deferred pensions (over and above any increases that may be required by law) that are on paper discretionary, but are in practice customarily granted as a measure of protection against inflation. The cost of such increases should be factored into both the annual current service cost (so that the cost is charged as it is earned through employees' service) and the measurement of the scheme liability at each year end.

21.3 An employer may in the past have granted occasional discretionary increases to pensions without creating an expectation of similar increases in the future. The cost of such increases would have resulted in additional past service liabilities (accounted for in accordance with paragraph 60) when they were granted. If the employer's practice changes such that a valid expectation of future increases is created, the future increases should also be provided for.

22   The benefits should be attributed to periods of service according to the scheme's benefit formula, except where the benefit formula attributes a disproportionate share of the total benefits to later years of service. In such cases, the benefit should be attributed on a straight-line basis over the period during which it is earned.

23   The assumptions underlying the valuation should be mutually compatible and lead to the best estimate of the future cash flows that will arise under the scheme liabilities. The assumptions are ultimately the responsibility of the directors (or equivalent) but should be set upon advice given by an actuary. Any assumptions that are affected by economic conditions (financial assumptions) should reflect market expectations at the balance sheet date.

24   Because of the long-term nature of most defined benefit schemes and the inherent uncertainties affecting them, the liabilities of the scheme are measured on an actuarial basis. This involves estimating the future cash flows arising under the scheme liabilities based on a number of actuarial assumptions such as mortality rates, employee turnover rates and salary growth, then discounting the cash flows at an appropriate rate.

25   Some of these assumptions are affected by the same economic factors. Actuarial assumptions are mutually compatible if they reflect the underlying economic factors consistently. To be consistent with the measurement of the assets of the scheme at fair value, they must also reflect market expectations at the balance sheet date.

26   For example, the rate of increase in salaries and the discount rate must reflect the same rate of general inflation. In jurisdictions where there is a liquid market in long-dated inflation-linked bonds, the yields on such bonds relative to those on fixed interest bonds of similar credit standing will give an indication of the expected rate of general inflation.

27   **The actuarial assumptions should reflect expected future events that will affect the cost of the benefits to which the employer is committed (either legally or through a constructive obligation) at the balance sheet date.**

28   Expected future events that will affect the cost of the benefits include:

(a)   any expected cost of living increases either provided for in the scheme rules, publicly announced or awarded under an established practice that creates among the employees a valid expectation of receiving them;

(b)   in the case of pensions based on final salary, any expected salary increases; and

(c)   expected early retirement where the employee has that right under the scheme rules.

These events affect the measurement of benefits to which the employer is committed at the balance sheet date.

29 Expected future redundancies are not reflected in the actuarial assumptions because the employer is not committed (either legally or constructively) to making such redundancies in advance. When the employer does become committed to making the redundancies, any impact on the defined benefit scheme is treated as a settlement and/or curtailment (see paragraph 64).

30 Expected future changes in the cost of retirement healthcare are particularly difficult to estimate—the cost often increases at a faster rate than either the retail price index or national earnings rate. Relevant considerations in determining the assumptions used to arrive at the retirement healthcare obligation include:

(a) advances in medical skills and technologies, often involving more expensive treatment;

(b) the rise in the expectations of prospective patients; and

(c) the effect of the above on companies, governments and insurance schemes in cutting back benefits, or making the patient pay a proportion.

31 It is not appropriate to assume a reduction in benefits below those currently promised on the grounds that the employer will curtail the scheme at some time in the future.

The discount rate

32 Defined benefit scheme liabilities should be discounted at a rate that reflects the time value of money and the characteristics of the liability. Such a rate should be assumed to be the current rate of return on a high quality corporate bond of equivalent currency and term to the scheme liabilities.

33   For this purpose, a high quality corporate bond means a bond that has been rated at the level of AA or equivalent status. The rate of return for such a bond reflects the time value of money and a small premium for risk. That premium is taken to reflect the options that the employer has to reduce the assumed scheme liabilities, including in extremis the option of closing down the scheme. If there is no liquid market in bonds of this type or duration, then a reasonable proxy should be used. This may be government bonds plus a margin for assumed credit risk spreads derived from global bond markets.

34   Many pension schemes provide benefits at least partly linked to inflation. One way to reflect that characteristic would be to consider the return on an index-linked corporate bond. However, given that there are few such bonds in existence, a more reliable alternative is to consider fixed interest corporate bonds and increase the cash flows to be discounted in line with inflation (ie project the liability to be discounted in nominal terms). Guidance on the inflation assumption is given in paragraph 26.

Frequency of valuations

35   Full actuarial valuations by a professionally qualified actuary should be obtained for a defined benefit scheme at intervals not exceeding three years. The actuary should review the most recent actuarial valuation at the balance sheet date and update it to reflect current conditions.

36   The actuarial valuations required for the FRS may use different assumptions and measurement methods from those used for a scheme's funding valuation. Full actuarial valuations under the FRS are not needed at every balance sheet date. Some aspects of the valuation will need to be updated at each balance sheet date, for example the fair value of the assets and financial assumptions such as the discount rate. Other assumptions, such as the expected

leaving rate and mortality rate, may not need to be updated annually.

36.1 In practice, it is likely that two full three-yearly actuarial valuations will be required for funded pension schemes: one for FRS 17 accounting and one for the pension scheme trustees. The FRS 17 valuation need not necessarily be done as at the company's balance sheet date. It could be done at an earlier date, or the same date as the valuation required by the trustees, as suits the company's reporting timetable. For example, a company with a December year end may have a pension scheme with a March year end and obtain actuarial valuations as at 31 March. The full valuation would then have to be updated to each company year end, including the one immediately following the date of the full valuation. The scheme assets should in any case be revalued at market values at each company balance sheet date. The scheme liabilities can, however, be estimated from the previous full valuation by rolling the valuation forward and updating it for changes to the scheme (such as benefit improvements) and in those assumptions that reflect changes in market conditions. Thus the discount rate should always be the current rate of return on the appropriate bond at the company's balance sheet date. A change in the discount rate may also require other financial assumptions, such as the inflation assumption, to be updated. The actuarial profession is developing guidance on the scope of the annual update.

Recognition of defined benefit schemes

Recognition in the balance sheet

37 **The surplus/deficit in a defined benefit scheme is the excess/shortfall of the value of the assets in the scheme over/below the present value of the scheme liabilities. The employer should recognise an asset to the extent that it is able to recover a surplus either through reduced contributions in the future or through refunds from the scheme. The employer**

should recognise a liability to the extent that it reflects its legal or constructive obligation.

38   A surplus in the scheme gives rise to an asset of the employer to the extent that:

(a) the employer controls its use, ie has the ability to use the surplus to generate future economic benefits for itself, either in the form of a reduction in future contributions or a refund from the scheme; and

(b) that control is a result of past events (contributions paid by the employer and investment growth in excess of rights earned by the employees).

Usually the employer's obligation under the trust deed is to pay such contributions as the actuary believes to be necessary to keep the scheme fully funded but without building up a surplus. When a surplus arises, it is unlikely that the employer can be required to make contributions to maintain the surplus. In addition, the award of benefit improvements is also usually in the hands of the employer. Thus, in general, the employer controls the use of a surplus in the scheme.

38.1 The FRS avoids implying that a surplus in a defined benefit pension scheme is 'owned' by the employer. But conceptually an employer does not have to own a surplus in order to recognise an asset. It is sufficient that the employer has access to future economic benefits that it controls *via*, for example, the ability to reduce future employer contributions.

39   Conversely, the employer has a liability if it has a legal or constructive obligation to make good a deficit in the defined benefit scheme. In general, the employer will either have a legal obligation under the terms of the scheme trust deed or will have by its past actions and statements created a constructive obligation

as defined in FRS 12 'Provisions, Contingent Liabilities and Contingent Assets'. The legal or constructive obligation to fund the deficit should be assumed to apply to the deficit based on assumptions used under the FRS.

40   In a scheme where employees as well as the employer make contributions, any deficit should be assumed to be borne by the employer unless the scheme rules require members' contributions to be increased to help fund a deficit. In this case, the present value of the required additional contributions should be treated as reducing the deficit to be recognised by the employer.

41   **In determining the asset to be recognised in accordance with paragraph 37, the amount that can be recovered through reduced contributions in the future is the present value of the liability expected to arise from future service by current and future scheme members less the present value of future employee contributions. No growth in the number of active scheme members should be assumed but a declining membership should be reflected if appropriate. The amount that can be recovered should be based on the assumptions used under the FRS, not the funding assumptions. The present value of the reduction in future contributions is determined using the discount rate applied to measure the defined benefit liability.**

42   **The amount to be recovered from refunds from the scheme should reflect only refunds that have been agreed by the pension scheme trustees at the balance sheet date.**

43   The employer may not control or be able to benefit from the whole of a surplus – it may be so large that the employer cannot absorb it all through reduced contributions, and refunds from the scheme may be difficult to obtain.

44   The amount recoverable through reduced contributions reflects the maximum possible to be recovered without assuming an increase in the number of employees covered by the scheme. There is no restriction on the period over which the reduction in contributions can be obtained, but the effect of discounting will increasingly reduce the impact of the reductions the further into the future they are, leading to an absolute limit on the amount that can be recognised.

44.1   In some situations, a surplus in a scheme may be so large that the scheme is in effect 'self-financing', because the return on assets exceeds the total of the current service cost and the interest cost on the scheme liabilities. If the surplus was recognised in an unrestricted way, a potentially ever-increasing asset could result (and corresponding credits in the profit and loss account), some of which could never be realised. The FRS caps the recognisable asset at the present value of a potential contribution holiday in perpetuity relating to a static or, if applicable, declining workforce. If the number of active members subsequently increases, the recoverable surplus may increase – paragraph 68 requires the increase to be credited to operating profit when it occurs.

44.2   Paragraph 41 makes it clear that the calculations of the recoverable accounting surplus should be based on the accounting assumptions rather than the funding assumptions, which may be more conservative. Paragraph 27 of Appendix IV discusses the apparent anomaly in situations where part of a surplus cannot be realised by the employer because of funding obligations agreed with the trustees, which may result in an accounting surplus being maintained indefinitely. The ASB argues that the financial statements should reflect the accounting surplus that is theoretically recoverable, irrespective of funding obligations that may actually limit the scope for reducing contributions, because over the life of the scheme the accounting and funding assumptions must come together. This result seems to be a natural consequence of using different accounting and funding assumptions – the accounting measurement rules might be inoperative if they were constrained by more conservative funding arrangements. Nevertheless, entities would need to consider the recoverability issue in the particular circumstances in which such assets arise.

44.3 A similar issue arises in relation to the minimum funding requirement (MFR) for defined benefit schemes that was introduced in the UK by the Pensions Act 1995 to protect the accrued rights of pension scheme members. The basis on which MFR is measured differs from the basis on which the scheme assets and liabilities are measured under the FRS. Schemes that are underfunded on a MFR basis have to achieve, *via* increased employer contributions, 100 per cent funding within five years. Situations may arise where a surplus measured on the FRS 17 basis could not be fully recovered by the employer because the statutory restriction would prevent employer contributions from being reduced below the level required to keep the scheme fully funded on an MFR basis. Depending on the particular circumstances, in some cases an entity may take the view that it cannot recover surplus if it is required to make contributions to maintain it.

45 In practice, a surplus that potentially could be recovered will instead often be used in part to provide benefit improvements to members, thereby reducing the amount that the employer recovers through reduced contributions. The use of a potentially recoverable surplus in this way should be treated as a past service cost when it occurs (see paragraph 60) and not anticipated by reducing the amount recognised as an asset.

45.1 Paragraph 21 explains, however, that where the scheme rules or an established pattern of past practice requires the employer to share a surplus with the members, the amount that will be passed to members should be treated as increasing the scheme liabilities. In these circumstances, any past service cost to which the employer is committed by virtue of a surplus would be anticipated in the recognition of a smaller surplus – and no past service cost would arise.

46   Paragraphs 67-70 specify how the limit on the amount that can be recognised as an asset should be recognised in the performance statements.

47   **Any unpaid contributions to the scheme should be presented in the balance sheet as a creditor due within one year. The defined benefit asset or liability should be presented separately on the face of the balance sheet:**

   (a) in balance sheets of the type prescribed for companies in Great Britain* by the Companies Act 1985, Schedule 4, format 1: after item J *Accruals and deferred income* but before item K *Capital and reserves;* and

   (b) in balance sheets of the type prescribed for companies in Great Britain by the Companies Act 1985, Schedule 4, format 2: any asset after ASSETS item D *Prepayments and accrued income* and any liability after LIABILITIES item D *Accruals and deferred income.*

   Where an employer has more than one scheme, the total of any defined benefit assets and the total of any defined benefit liabilities should be shown separately on the face of the balance sheet.

48   An example of the required presentation for the defined benefit asset or liability other than any unpaid contributions is shown in Appendix I.

48.1 The method of calculating the surplus or deficit will often lead to large variations in the 'pension balance' year on year. Market values of the scheme assets will fluctuate, as will the present value of the

---

* *The equivalent statutory provisions for Northern Ireland are in the Companies (Northern Ireland) Order 1986, Schedule 4; and for the Republic of Ireland are in the Companies (Amendment) Act 1986, the Schedule.*

scheme liabilities, not least from applying different discount rates to the gross liability. But at least the pension balance will be a number that has some meaning for most readers and it will be clearly visible as a separate category on the face of the balance sheet. The FRS makes no suggestion that this adaptation of the balance sheet formats contained in Schedule 4 of the Companies Act 1985 involves a true and fair override of those formats.

49   The deferred tax relating to the defined benefit asset or liability should be offset against the defined benefit asset or liability and not included with other deferred tax assets or liabilities.

Recognition in the performance statements

50   The change in the defined benefit asset or liability (other than that arising from contributions to the scheme) should be analysed into the following components:

Periodic costs

(a)   the current service cost;

(b)   the interest cost;

(c)   the expected return on assets;

(d)   actuarial gains and losses;

Non-periodic costs

(e)   past service costs; and

(f)   gains and losses on settlements and curtailments.

Current service cost, interest cost and expected return on assets

51 **The current service cost should be based on the most recent actuarial valuation at the beginning of the period, with the financial assumptions updated to reflect conditions at that date. It should be included within operating profit in the profit and loss account (except insofar as the related employee remuneration is capitalised in accordance with another accounting standard). Any contributions from employees should be set off against the current service cost.**

52   The current service cost will be based on the discount rate at the beginning of the period and will therefore reflect current long-term market interest rates at that time.

52.1   Current service cost represents the actuarially calculated present value of the pension benefits earned by the active employees in each period. It is supposed to reflect the true economic cost relating to each year. This cost is determined independently of the funding of the scheme. In principle, therefore, for a given set of employees and benefit formulae, the current service cost (shown as an operating cost) should be the same irrespective of whether the scheme is in surplus, in deficit or unfunded. Unlike SSAP 24's regular cost, the current service cost is not necessarily a stable percentage of pensionable pay year on year. For example, current service cost will vary if the discount rate changes. It will increase year on year as a proportion of pay if the average age of the workforce is increasing, as is likely where the scheme is closed to new entrants.

53 **The interest cost should be based on the discount rate and the present value of the scheme liabilities at the beginning of the period. The interest cost should, in addition, reflect changes in the scheme liabilities during the period.**

53.1   The interest cost represents the unwinding of the discount on the scheme liabilities. As for the current service cost, the interest cost is determined independently of the funding of the scheme. The discount rate applicable to any financial year, being the appropriate high quality corporate bond rate at the beginning of the year, is the same as the rate at which the scheme liabilities are measured at the end of the previous year. The interest cost needs to reflect an average of the liability at the beginning of the year and movements during the year. For example, the current service cost, past service costs relating to benefit improvements and transfers into the scheme will increase the liability during the year; benefits paid to pensioners and transfers out of the scheme will reduce the liability during the year.

54   The expected return on assets is based on long-term expectations at the beginning of the period and is expected to be reasonably stable. For quoted corporate or government bonds, the expected return should be calculated by applying the current redemption yield at the beginning of the period to the market value of the bonds held by the scheme at the beginning of the period. For other assets (for example, equities), the expected return should be calculated by applying the rate of return expected over the long term at the beginning of the period (given the value of the assets at that date) to the fair value of the assets held by the scheme at the beginning of the period. The expected return on assets should, in addition, reflect changes in the assets in the scheme during the period as a result of contributions paid into and benefits paid out of the scheme. The expected rate of return should be set by the directors (or equivalent) having taken advice from an actuary.

55   For quoted fixed and index-linked securities, the expected return can be observed from the market. For other assets, the expected return has to be based on assumptions about the expected long-term rate of return. The rate of return expected over the long term will vary according to market conditions, but it is expected that the amount of the return will be reasonably stable.

55.1   This component of the pension cost reflects the funding of a scheme. The profit and loss account is credited each period with the expected long-term rate of return on the assets, based on their market values at the beginning of the year. Where applicable – for example, equities and properties – the rate of return will include expected capital growth as well as income from dividends and rents. The treatment in the employer company's profit and loss account is, therefore, unrelated to the realisation of income and capital gains in the pension scheme itself. The scheme assets are revalued to fair value at each balance sheet date. The difference between the fair value and the 'expected' value of the assets – that is, the value that has accrued by crediting the expected rate of return – is recognised as an actuarial gain or loss in the STRGL (see paragraph 57). Thus the amount credited each year in the profit and loss account should be a relatively stable long-term return, whereas short-term volatility in equity and other asset values is shown in the STRGL.

55.2   The expected rate of return has to be estimated for each significant class of asset. For each class, the calculation needs to reflect an average of the market value at the beginning of the year and movements during the year – for example, contributions received, pensions paid and transfers of assets in and out. Assumptions need to be made about where contributions are invested and from where benefit payments are sourced. The FRS does not require changes during the year in the portfolio mix or risk profile to be taken into account in the calculations, so the effect of such changes would in general be reflected as actuarial gains or losses reported in the STRGL rather than as adjustments to the expected long-term rate of return reported in the profit and loss account. However, if the pension scheme trustees significantly changed the risk profile of the portfolio mid-year (for example, making a significant switch from equities to bonds), it might be appropriate for the calculations to reflect this.

56   The net of the interest cost and the expected return on assets should be included as other finance costs (or income) adjacent to interest.

56.1 The net figure in the profit and loss account is affected by how the scheme is funded. It will be a net credit if the expected return on the scheme assets exceeds the interest cost on the scheme liabilities. This is likely to occur if a scheme is in surplus on the accounting measurement basis and/or if a higher rate of return is applied to the scheme assets than the discount rate applied to the scheme liabilities. A higher rate of return on assets is inherent in the basis on which the respective rates are calculated – for example, any expected equity risk premium relating to an equity portfolio is reflected in the investment return, but is precluded from being recognised in the interest cost. As UK schemes hold a majority of scheme assets in equities, the profit and loss account will benefit from equities' expected long-term out-performance of bonds.

56.2 The note on legal requirements (paragraph 6 of Appendix II) makes it clear that paragraph 56 introduces a new format heading 'other finance costs (or income)' into the profit and loss account. This new heading should be shown adjacent to, but separate from, 'interest payable and similar charges'. Paragraph 84 requires the two components of this item to be disclosed separately in the notes. Furthermore, paragraph 102 amends paragraph 48 of FRS 12 by requiring that for all long-term provisions covered by FRS 12 that are measured at a present value (such as decommissioning liabilities), the unwinding of the discount (equivalent to the interest cost relating to pension liabilities) should be shown under this new separate format heading. Previously, the unwinding of the discount on provisions could be shown either separately on the face of the profit and loss account (adjacent to interest) or it could be included in the heading 'interest payable and similar charges' on the face of the profit and loss account and be disclosed in a note as a separate component of that heading. However, the requirement to disclose interest costs on other provisions under the new format heading does not apply until the accounting requirements of FRS 17 itself are adopted.

Actuarial gains and losses

57 Actuarial gains and losses arising from any new valuation and from updating the latest actuarial valuation to reflect

conditions at the balance sheet date should be recognised in the statement of total recognised gains and losses for the period.

58   Actuarial gains and losses may arise on both the defined benefit scheme liabilities and any scheme assets. They comprise:

(a) on the scheme assets, differences between the expected return and the actual return (for example, a sudden change in the value of the scheme assets);

(b) on the scheme liabilities, (i) differences between the actuarial assumptions underlying the scheme liabilities and actual experience during the period and (ii) the effect of changes in actuarial assumptions; and

(c) any adjustment necessary in accordance with paragraph 67 resulting from the limit on the amount that can be recognised as an asset in the balance sheet.

59   Once an actuarial gain or loss has been recognised in the statement of total recognised gains and losses it is not recognised again in the profit and loss account in subsequent periods.

59.1 Actuarial gains and losses arise from unexpected increases or decreases in the fair value of the scheme assets or the present value of the scheme liabilities, including the effects of changes in assumptions. The expected increase in the fair value of scheme assets is recognised in the profit and loss account (see paragraph 54). The difference between the expected and actual return is treated as an actuarial gain or loss and is recognised in the STRGL. Actuarial gains and losses relating to the scheme liabilities will result from factors such as unexpectedly high or low rates of employee turnover, early retirements or mortality; unexpected changes in salaries or medical costs; and changes in the discount rate.

Past service costs

60 **Past service costs should be recognised in the profit and loss account on a straight-line basis over the period in which the increases in benefit vest. To the extent that the benefits vest immediately, the past service cost should be recognised immediately. Any unrecognised past service costs should be deducted from the scheme liabilities and the balance sheet asset or liability adjusted accordingly.**

61 Past service costs arise when the employer makes a commitment to provide a higher level of benefit than previously promised, for example the creation of a pension benefit for a spouse where such a benefit did not previously exist or a grant of early retirement with added-on years of service.

62 Past service costs do not include increases in the expected cost of benefits that the employer is already statutorily, contractually or implicitly committed to, for example cost of living increases to pensions in payment and deferred pensions. Such increases are covered by the actuarial assumptions and any difference between actual experience and the assumptions or the effects of any changes in the assumptions are actuarial gains and losses.

63 Past service costs include benefit improvements awarded as a result of a surplus arising in the scheme. The fact that they are funded out of a surplus does not result in there being no cost to the employer if the surplus was potentially recoverable by the employer – the use of the surplus for benefit improvements means that the employer cannot then benefit from it in other ways.

63.1 Benefit improvements may produce both an increase in the cost of future service relating to active members (reflected in a higher annual current service cost) and an increased liability for past service relating to current and ex-employees. Unlike SSAP 24, the cost (that is, the capitalised present value) of the element of all benefit improvements that relates to past service and that have not previously been allowed for in the valuation of the scheme liabilities should be charged to the profit and loss account over the vesting period. Often the improvements will vest immediately they are granted. This treatment applies irrespective of whether the additional past service liability relates to pensioners, deferred pensioners or current employees, or whether the benefit improvements are funded by surplus or give rise to a deficiency.

63.2   It should be noted, however, that where the scheme rules or an established pattern of past practice requires the employer to share a surplus with the members, the amount that will be passed to members (probably as a benefit improvement) should be treated as increasing the scheme liabilities (see paragraph 21). In these circumstances, any past service cost to which the employer is committed by virtue of a surplus would already have been anticipated in the recognition of a smaller surplus and gain – and no past service cost would arise.

63.3   It should be noted that the definition of 'retirement benefits' in paragraph 2 specifically excludes benefits that become payable as a result of the early termination of an employee's employment. Therefore, where employees made redundant are granted enhanced pension benefits (say, for early retirement) *in lieu* of, or in addition to, redundancy payments, the cost of the enhanced pension benefits are in effect treated as redundancy payments rather than past service costs. Some such benefits might relate to the termination of an operation or fundamental reorganisation and be shown as FRS 3 paragraph 20 items outside operating profit.

Settlements and curtailments

64   Losses arising on a settlement or curtailment not allowed for in the actuarial assumptions should be measured at the date on which the employer becomes demonstrably committed to the transaction and recognised in the profit and loss account covering that date. Gains arising on a settlement or curtailment not allowed for in the actuarial assumptions should be measured at the date on which all parties whose

consent is required are irrevocably committed to the transaction and recognised in the profit and loss account covering that date.

65   Where under the scheme rules the employees have the option to retire early or transfer out of the scheme, the resulting settlements and curtailments are allowed for in the normal demographic assumptions made by the actuary and any gains and losses arising are actuarial gains and losses.

66   In contrast, some settlements and curtailments arise from specific decisions made by an employer that are not covered by actuarial assumptions, for example major changes in the circumstances of the scheme instigated by the employer, such as the transfer of accrued benefits of some or all the members into a defined contribution scheme or a reduction in employees because of the sale or termination of an operation. Gains and losses arising from such events are part of the employer's operating results for the period (unless they attach to one of the items shown immediately after operating profit).

66.1 Settlements and curtailments are events that materially change the liabilities relating to a scheme and that are not covered by the normal actuarial assumptions. Settlements have the effect of extinguishing a portion of the scheme liabilities, usually by transferring scheme assets to or on behalf of scheme members – for example, when a subsidiary is sold or when assets and liabilities are transferred into a defined contribution scheme. Curtailments have the effect of reducing the obligations relating to future service, usually as a result of a significant reduction in the number of employees – for example, on the termination of an operation – or as a result of a reduction in future benefits – for example, following an amendment to the rules.

66.2 Calculating the gain or loss arising from a settlement or curtailment event requires a 'before' and 'after' measurement. The gain or loss is in principle the resulting change in the surplus or deficit (that is, the scheme assets less the scheme liabilities) attributable to the reporting entity.

66.3 Paragraph 64 specifies the date when the employer should measure and recognise the gain or loss arising. The measurement may not be straightforward. It is unfortunate, from a practical viewpoint, that the measurement dates are potentially different for gains and losses since, until the scheme is valued, it may not be certain whether a gain or a loss has arisen. Furthermore, the FRS does not specify whether the surplus or deficit at the measurement date should be measured using the actuarial assumptions at the beginning of the year (for example, the discount rate for liabilities) or at the later measurement date. Nor does not it indicate whether the scheme assets should be valued at their fair values at the measurement date or at their expected values derived from their fair values at the beginning of the year. This issue is relevant because for both assets and liabilities, unrecorded actuarial gains or losses may have occurred between the beginning of the year and the measurement date. How the calculation is performed will affect the allocation of total gains and losses during the year between those relating to the settlement or curtailment event (reported in the profit and loss account) and other actuarial gains and losses (reported in the STRGL).

66.4 IAS 19 is more specific and requires the employer to re-measure the scheme liability and scheme assets using current actuarial assumptions. This means that a new discount rate should be used to measure the change in liabilities if the discount rate has changed since the beginning of the year, and current market prices should be used to measure the change in assets. This approach makes sense, because the gain or loss attributed to the settlement or curtailment event is then based on fair values at the date of such event.

66.5 Where a subsidiary or other operation is sold, it should be remembered that any pre-existing surplus or deficiency relating to that subsidiary will already have been recognised in the consolidated financial statements of the parent (although not in the subsidiary if it is using defined contribution accounting in respect of a group scheme). If the surplus or deficiency is transferred to the purchaser, a corresponding settlement loss or gain will be reflected in the calculation of the profit or loss on disposal of the subsidiary, since it forms part of the attributable net assets disposed of.

Impact of limit on balance sheet asset

67   **The limit set out in paragraph 41 on the amount that can be recognised as an asset may result in there being some part of a defined benefit scheme surplus that is not recognised. Where this is the case, the amounts recognised in the performance statements should be adjusted as follows.**

(a)   **First, if any refund is agreed and is covered by the unrecognised surplus, it should be recognised as other finance income adjacent to interest, with separate disclosure in the notes.**

Refunds from schemes where the whole surplus is regarded as recoverable do not give rise to gains. The cash received simply reduces the balance sheet asset (along with any related tax effect).

(b)   **Next, the unrecognised surplus should be applied to extinguish past service costs or losses on settlements or curtailments that would otherwise be charged in the profit and loss account for the period, with disclosure in the notes of the items and amounts so extinguished.**

(c)   **Next, the expected return on assets should be restricted so that it does not exceed the total of the current service cost, interest cost (and any past service costs and losses on settlements and curtailments not covered by the unrecognised surplus) and any increase in the recoverable surplus.**

(d)   **Finally, any further adjustment necessary should be treated as an actuarial gain or loss.**

67.1 The basic recognition rule in paragraph 37 means that the amount of surplus recognised as an asset should not exceed the present value of the amounts that the employer can recover through potential contribution holidays and agreed refunds. Where an asset is restricted in this way, the opening and closing balance sheet figures are determined by calculating the maximum recoverable amount of surplus, using the assumptions specified in paragraphs 41 and 42.

67.2 The rules for measuring the impact of restricting the asset on the components in the performance statements are complex. The existence of an unrecognised surplus may result in there being no net cost to the employer during the year, but the separate debit and credit components in the profit and loss account have to be measured and disclosed on a systematic basis. Many different scenarios are possible, as illustrated in the following examples.

67.3 The following table illustrates the simple case where a recognised surplus is the same at the beginning and end of the year, no past service benefits are awarded, no curtailments or settlements occur, no actuarial gains or losses arise in the scheme and no employer contributions are paid during the year.

	Surplus in scheme	Recoverable surplus and P&L account
Surplus at beginning of year	350	180
Current service cost	(20)	(20)
Interest cost	(25)	(25)
Expected return on assets	60	45
Net finance income	35	20
Net pension credit	15	Nil
Surplus at end of year	365	180

The 'surplus in scheme' column shows the actual surplus in the scheme and the components of performance before any restriction on the asset. The surplus in the scheme has increased by 15 from

350 to 365, but the recognised surplus is restricted to 180 at the beginning and end of the year.

This example illustrates that the system set out in paragraph 67 works as follows.

- Current service cost (operating charge) is unaffected by the existence of the surplus. It cannot be offset under any circumstances.

- Interest cost is calculated as normal on the gross amount of the scheme liability.

- Expected return on scheme assets absorbs the effect of the irrecoverable surplus. In the example, the expected return on the gross assets in the scheme is 60. The credit recognised in the profit and loss account is restricted so that it does not exceed the current service cost and interest cost in aggregate, that is 45.

- The overall profit and loss charge is nil. No further adjustment is necessary in the STRGL. The actual surplus in the scheme has increased by 15, but that increases the irrecoverable (unrecognised) surplus.

67.4 The following table adds some more features and becomes more complex. At the beginning of the year benefit improvements were granted out of the surplus, which vested immediately, giving a past service cost of 200. At the end of the year the recoverable surplus was estimated to have increased to 190 as a result of a reduced discount rate; the actual surplus in the scheme was valued at 210. The amounts recognised in the performance statements are shown below. The first column shows the amounts as if the surplus in the scheme was recognised in full. The second column shows the restricted amounts recognised in the employer's financial statements.

	Surplus in scheme	Recoverable surplus and components of performance
Surplus at beginning of year	350	180
Current service cost	(20)	(20)
Past service cost (gross)	(200)	(200)
Less: unrecognised surplus	–	170
Past service cost (net)	(200)	(30)
Operating cost	(220)	(50)
Interest cost	(25)	(25)
Expected return on assets	60	60
Net finance income	35	35
Net pension cost (P&L)	(185)	(15)
Actuarial gain (STRGL)	45	25
Surplus at end of year	210	190

First, in calculating the past service cost to the company, credit is taken for the previously unrecognised surplus in the scheme. Therefore, the gross past service cost of 200 is reduced by 170 (that is, total scheme surplus 350 less surplus already recognised on the balance sheet 180). The separate components of the net past service cost of 30 do not have to be shown on the face of the profit and loss account, but paragraph 82 requires them to be disclosed in the notes. As noted earlier, the current service cost cannot be reduced in this way.

Secondly, the expected return on the scheme assets is 60. The amount credited in the profit and loss account cannot exceed the total of the current service cost (20), interest cost (25) and the net past service cost (30). As the total of these amounts exceeds the expected return on the actual scheme assets, no restriction is required.

Thirdly, any further adjustment necessary to increase the recoverable surplus should be credited in the STRGL as an actuarial gain. In this example there is an actuarial gain of 45 in the valuation of the surplus in the scheme. In the company's financial statements an actuarial gain of 25 is recognised in the STRGL, bringing the recognised asset to 190.

68   An increase in the recoverable amount of a surplus arising from an increase in the active membership of the scheme should be recognised as an operating gain.

69   An increase in the active membership can arise either from an increase in general recruitment or from the transfer of employees following an acquisition. The gain arising in the latter case is a post-acquisition operating gain, not an adjustment to the purchase price and goodwill.

69.1   The rule in paragraph 41 means that a pension asset recognised by the employer cannot exceed the present value of a potential contribution holiday in perpetuity relating to a static (or, if applicable, declining) number of active scheme members. No increase in the number of active scheme members can be anticipated in the calculation of the recoverable surplus at each year end. Therefore, where a scheme has a surplus that is partly unrecognised by the employer, the recoverable amount of the surplus is likely to increase year on year if there is an increase in the number of active members. The FRS requires the portion of any increase in recoverable surplus that is attributable to an increase in the number of active members to be shown as an operating gain.

69.2   An acquisition could give rise to an increase in the active membership of the acquirer's scheme. This might occur where employees of the acquired business are transferred to the acquirer's scheme and assets are transferred reflecting transfer values of their accrued pension benefits. In these circumstances, whilst there may be no increase in the surplus in the acquirer's scheme resulting from the transfer, the portion that is deemed to be recoverable may increase. A similar effect may occur where a scheme in an acquired group is merged with the acquirer's scheme. Consistent with FRS 7, the effect of such changes should be reflected in the acquirer's post-acquisition results rather than as adjustments in the fair value exercise.

70 **A decrease in the recoverable amount of a surplus arising from a fall in the active membership should be treated as an actuarial loss unless it arises from an event not covered by the assumptions underlying the amount originally regarded as recoverable, for example a settlement or curtailment. If it does arise from such an event, it should be treated as part of the loss arising on that event.**

Tax

71 **When current tax relief arises on contributions made to a defined benefit scheme, it should be allocated to the profit and loss account or statement of total recognised gains and losses on the basis that the contribution covers first the items reported in the profit and loss account and then any actuarial losses reported in the statement of total recognised gains and losses, unless it is clear that some other allocation is more appropriate. To the extent that the contribution exceeds these items, the current tax relief attributable to the excess should be allocated to the profit and loss account, again unless it is clearly more appropriate to allocate it to the statement of total recognised gains and losses.**

72   Current tax relief is usually available on contributions paid to the scheme and deferred tax usually arises on the balance of the charges/credits. The tax follows the relevant item, ie tax on the service cost, interest cost and expected return on assets will be recognised in the profit and loss account and tax on the actuarial gains and losses will be recognised in the statement of total recognised gains and losses. FRS 16 'Current Tax' requires disclosure of the current tax recognised in the profit and loss account and statement of total recognised gains and losses. The question arises of where the current tax relief arising on contributions should be deemed to belong. Sometimes it will be clear what the contribution relates to, for example when a special contribution is made to fund a deficit arising from an identifiable

cause, say an actuarial loss, in which case the current tax relief should be allocated to the statement of total recognised gains and losses. In the absence of a clear link between the contribution and the items recognised in the performance statements, the allocation in paragraph 71 should be followed.

72.1 In the UK, tax relief on employers' pension contributions is usually given in the period in which they are paid rather than when the costs are recognised in the accounts. In an unfunded scheme, and in the case of provisions for unfunded benefits such as post-retirement healthcare, the tax relief is given when the pensions or other benefits are paid. Where the total of the pension costs recognised under FRS 17 differs from the actual contributions (or unfunded benefits) paid, the resulting asset or liability recognised in the balance sheet is a timing difference for deferred tax purposes.

72.2 The timing difference that originates in one period is capable of reversing in one or more subsequent periods, albeit possibly over a relatively long time scale. For example, an actuarial gain in the current period does not increase taxable profits until pension contributions are reduced in future periods – when that happens, taxable profits will in effect reflect a portion of the gain that has previously been recognised in the accounts. Under FRS 19, deferred tax should be provided in full on all timing differences that have originated but not reversed by the balance sheet date; deferred tax assets (which relate to liabilities recognised under FRS 17) should be recognised to the extent that they are regarded as recoverable.

72.3 Under FRS 17, various components of pension cost are reported in the profit and loss account; actuarial gains and losses are reported in the STRGL. So in any period, pension cost accounting may give rise to current tax (tax relief on contributions) and deferred tax (on the timing differences between contributions and costs). FRS 16 requires current tax to be recognised in the profit and loss account, except where it is attributable to a gain or loss that has been recognised directly in the STRGL, in which case the attributable tax should also be recognised directly in the STRGL. Similarly, FRS 19 requires deferred tax to be recognised in the profit and loss account, except where it is attributable to a gain or loss that has been recognised directly in the STRGL. Normally, there is no direct relationship between the components of pension cost reported in the performance statements and the contributions and benefits paid in a period, and so paragraph 71 specifies a hierarchy for allocating current tax between the profit and loss account and the STRGL. Deferred tax will normally arise on the balance of costs and credits in each statement.

72.4 The allocation of current and deferred tax is illustrated in the following table, which shows the movements in a surplus during the year. A tax rate of 30 per cent is assumed.

	Change in defined benefit asset	Current tax relief (30%)	Deferred tax (30%)
Asset b/f	120		(36)
Contributions	70	21	
P&L – net pension cost	(60)	18	--
STRGL – actuarial loss	(20)	3	3
	(80)	21	3
Asset c/f	110	–	(33)

Current tax relief arises on contributions paid of 70. This is allocated first to cover the pension cost of 60 reported in the profit and loss account (resulting in a credit of 18 in the tax charge in the profit and loss account). The balance of the contributions paid, 10, is allocated to the actuarial loss and hence current tax of 3 is credited in the STRGL. Deferred tax of 3 is attributable to the balance of the actuarial loss, 10, and is credited in the STRGL.

Note that paragraph 49 requires the deferred tax to be offset against the defined benefit asset in the balance sheet.

72.5 If, in the above example, there was an actuarial gain rather than an actuarial loss, the whole of the current tax relief of 21 would be credited in the profit and loss account, and deferred tax attributable to the actuarial gain would be charged in the STRGL, as illustrated below.

	Change in defined benefit asset	Current tax relief (30%)	Deferred tax (30%)
Asset b/f	120		(36)
Contributions	70	21	
P&L – net pension cost	(60)	21	(3)
STRGL – actuarial gain	20	–	(6)
	(40)	21	(9)
Asset c/f	150	–	(45)

72.6   FRS 16 requires the current tax charged or credited in the profit and loss account and the STRGL to be disclosed separately; FRS 19 requires the deferred tax charged or credited in the profit and loss account and the STRGL to be disclosed separately.

Death-in-service and incapacity benefits

73   A charge should be made to operating profit to reflect the expected cost of providing any death-in-service or incapacity benefits for the period. Any difference between that expected cost and amounts actually incurred should be treated as an actuarial gain or loss.

74   Where a scheme insures the death-in-service costs, the expected cost for the accounting period is simply the premium payable for the period. Where the costs are not insured, the expected cost reflects the probability of any employees dying in the period and the benefit that would then be paid out.

74.1   An accrual is required for the annual cost of providing death-in-service benefits even if the benefits are uninsured. This is consistent with how the pension liability is calculated, as it will be reduced to reflect actuarial assumptions about deaths in service.

Disclosures

Defined contribution schemes

75   The following disclosures should be made in respect of a
     defined contribution scheme:

   (a) the nature of the scheme (ie defined contribution);

   (b) the cost for the period; and

   (c) any outstanding or prepaid contributions at the balance
        sheet date.

Defined benefit schemes

76   The following disclosures should be made in respect of a
     defined benefit scheme:

   (a) the nature of the scheme (ie defined benefit);

   (b) the date of the most recent full actuarial valuation on
        which the amounts in the financial statements are based.
        If the actuary is an employee or officer of the reporting
        entity, or of the group of which it is a member, this fact
        should be disclosed;

   (c) the contribution made in respect of the accounting period
        and any agreed contribution rates for future years; and

   (d) for closed schemes and those in which the age profile of
        the active membership is rising significantly, the fact that
        under the projected unit method the current service cost
        will increase as the members of the scheme approach
        retirement.

77   Paragraph 9 requires additional disclosures about some multi-employer defined benefit schemes that are accounted for as if they were defined contribution schemes.

Assumptions

78   Each of the main financial assumptions used at the beginning of the period and at the balance sheet date should be disclosed. They should be disclosed as separate individual figures, not combined or netted. The main financial assumptions include:

    (a) the inflation assumption;

    (b) the rate of increase in salaries;

    (c) the rate of increase for pensions in payment and deferred pensions; and

    (d) the rate used to discount scheme liabilities.

79   The most important assumptions underlying the present value of the scheme liabilities are the rates of increase in salaries and pensions in payment and the rate of interest applied to discount the estimated cash flows arising under the liabilities. The valuation of assets in the scheme is not affected by the actuarial assumptions because the assets are measured at fair value.

Fair value and expected return on assets

80   The fair value of the assets held by the pension scheme at the beginning and end of the period should be analysed into the following classes and disclosed together with the expected rate of return assumed for each class for the period and the subsequent period:

(a) **equities;**

(b) **bonds; and**

(c) **other (subanalysed if material).**

81 The assumption made for the expected return on assets does not affect the valuation of the scheme assets because they are measured at fair value. It does, however, determine the amount to be recognised in the profit and loss account.

81.1 Users can be expected to pay considerable attention to assumed rates of return on scheme assets, since they determine the amount of investment income that is credited in the profit and loss account. The differences between actual and assumed expected rates of return pass through the STRGL. Users will be able to spot if one company appears to be out of line with others as regards the expected rates of return that have been assumed. The expected rates of return assumed for the subsequent period do not affect any of the figures in the current period's financial statements (as these figures are based on last year's closing expected rates of return), but they are important assumptions relating to next year's profit and loss account. The requirement to disclose them up front prevents those important assumptions from being manipulated with hindsight in the following year.

Components of the defined benefit cost

82 **The following amounts included within operating profit (or capitalised with the relevant employee remuneration) should be disclosed in the notes to the financial statements:**

(a) **the current service cost;**

(b) **any past service costs;**

(c) any previously unrecognised surplus deducted from the past service costs;

(d) gains and losses on any settlements or curtailments; and

(e) any previously unrecognised surplus deducted from the settlement or curtailment losses.

83   Any gains and losses on settlements or curtailments (and any previously unrecognised surplus deducted from the losses) included within a separate item after operating profit should be disclosed in the notes to the financial statements.

84   The following amounts included as other finance costs (or income) should be disclosed separately in the notes to the financial statements:

(a) the interest cost; and

(b) the expected return on assets in the scheme.

85   The following amounts included within the statement of total recognised gains and losses should be disclosed in the notes to the financial statements:

(a) the difference between the expected and actual return on assets;

(b) experience gains and losses arising on the scheme liabilities; and

(c) the effects of changes in the demographic and financial assumptions underlying the present value of the scheme liabilities.

History of amounts recognised in the statement of total recognised gains and losses

86 The notes to the financial statements should disclose, for the accounting period and previous four periods:

(a) the difference between the expected and actual return on assets expressed as (i) an amount and (ii) a percentage of the scheme assets at the balance sheet date;

(b) the experience gains and losses arising on the scheme liabilities expressed as (i) an amount and (ii) a percentage of the present value of the scheme liabilities at the balance sheet date; and

(c) the total actuarial gain or loss expressed as (i) an amount and (ii) a percentage of the present value of the scheme liabilities at the balance sheet date.

87 A consistent trend of experience losses/gains in the statement of total recognised gains and losses may indicate that the assumptions used have been over-optimistic/over-pessimistic and may cast doubt upon the reliability of the amounts reported in the profit and loss account. Where such a trend has emerged it is important that careful consideration is given to the choice of assumptions in the future.

87.1 Paragraph 96 of the FRS does not require the five-year history of amounts recognised in the STRGL to be created retrospectively when the FRS is adopted in full. Under the transitional arrangements in paragraph 94, these disclosures are required from the second transitional year, that is from June 2002 year ends, and so the five-year record will not be complete until 2006.

87.2 As indicated in paragraph 87, the purpose of these disclosures is to monitor and expose the reasonableness of the annual assumptions underlying the pension cost figures that pass through the profit and loss account. Differences between the expected costs that pass through the profit and loss account and actual history pass through the STRGL as actuarial gains and losses. A continuing trend of debits or credits in the STRGL could open the actuarial assumptions to challenge.

87.3 It should be noted that, for amounts passed through the STRGL in respect of the scheme liabilities, paragraphs 85 (b) and (c) require experience gains and losses and the effect of changes in actuarial assumptions to be disclosed separately in the notes. However, the disclosure in 86(b) relating to the five-year history refers only to experience gains and losses and does not include gains and losses relating to changes in assumptions, as illustrated in the example in Appendix I to the FRS.

Reconciliation to the balance sheet

88 **The fair value of the scheme assets, the present value of the scheme liabilities based on the accounting assumptions and the resulting surplus or deficit should be disclosed in a note to the financial statements. Where the asset or liability in the balance sheet differs from the surplus or deficit in the scheme, an explanation of the difference should be given. An analysis of the movements during the period in the surplus or deficit in the scheme should be given.**

89 Differences between the asset or liability in the balance sheet and the surplus or deficit in the scheme will arise because of the related deferred tax balance and also when part of a surplus or deficit has not been recognised in the balance sheet, for example when part of the surplus in the scheme is not recoverable by the employer or when past service awards have not yet vested.

89.1 Paragraph 89 describes the only circumstances where the asset or liability recognised in the employer's balance sheet (before attributable deferred tax) should differ from the surplus or deficit in the scheme as measured under the FRS, because in all other circumstances the surplus or deficit should be recognised in full.

Paragraph 60 specifies the circumstances where past service costs should be spread forward.

Example

Fair value of scheme assets	350
Present value of scheme liabilities	(150)
Surplus in the scheme	200
Less: past service costs not yet vested	(20)
	180
Less: irrecoverable surplus	(40)
Recognised pension asset	140
Related deferred tax liability	(42)
Net pension asset	98

Analysis of reserves

90   The analysis of reserves in the notes to the financial statements should distinguish the amount relating to the defined benefit asset or liability net of the related deferred tax.

90.1   Pension items find their way into reserves *via* the profit and loss account (components of pension cost) and STRGL (actuarial gains and losses). The FRS does not specify to which reserves amounts passed through the STRGL should be debited or credited. The disclosure example in Appendix 1 to the FRS indicates a pension asset that is reflected in its entirety in the profit and loss reserve (net of attributable deferred tax). Some may prefer to take the cumulative actuarial gains to a separate pension reserve.

90.2   In practice, a pension asset or liability will often arise from better or worse than expected investment performance or other actuarial gains and losses. But this will not be the only reason. An asset will arise in acquisition accounting where the acquired entity has a pension scheme in surplus. Similarly, a deficit (or unfunded liability) may have arisen as part of accounting for an acquisition. More generally, in a funded scheme, the amount of contribution payments will affect the composition of any asset or liability. A recognised asset or liability is normally attributable to shareholders – and, hence, in a broad sense, reflected in capital and reserves. An exception is where, in consolidated financial statements, part of the asset or liability relates to minority interests in a subsidiary. Where a defined benefit scheme is operated by a less than wholly-owned subsidiary, the whole of the surplus or deficit is recognised as an asset or liability in the consolidated balance sheet, but only the group's share is reflected in shareholders' funds (the minority's share being reflected in minority interests). Consequently, properly speaking, only the group's share of the defined benefit asset or liability would be disclosed under paragraph 90.

Distributable reserves

90.3   The FRS is silent on the question whether pension assets and liabilities give rise to realised or unrealised gains and losses. The issue only arises in respect of assets and liabilities recognised in the financial statements of individual companies, not groups. FRED 20 had noted the ASB's view that the immediate recognition of actuarial gains and losses does not affect their realisation, but that under sections 264 and 270 of the Companies Act, the recognition of a deficit as a liability might affect the ability of a public company to make a distribution (because public companies must take into account unrealised losses). The FRED had proposed a method of splitting a pension deficit between the part that represented a deficit on a discontinuance basis (deemed to be a realised loss) and the balance that resulted from measuring the deficit on a projected unit method (deemed to be an unrealised loss). However, that approach has been abandoned in the FRS, as explained in Appendix IV, paragraph 58.

90.4   Appendix IV, paragraph 58 indicates that a distribution problem will arise only where individual company financial statements show a deficit so large that it reduces distributable reserves to below that needed to cover any intended distribution. We believe that this should be construed as applying to all companies and not just public companies. Unless a company receives legal advice to the contrary, there should be a working presumption that cumulative actuarial gains give rise to an *unrealised* profit and cumulative actuarial losses give rise to a *realised* loss.

90.5 The possibilities of an unexpected decline in distributable profits are mitigated, however, by FRS 17's rules relating to group defined benefit schemes (see paragraphs 9-12). Where a scheme that covers more than one company does not enable the individual companies to identify their share of the scheme's assets and liabilities, the FRS requires each company (including the parent) to treat the scheme as a defined contribution scheme. Each individual company should, therefore, recognise only the employer contributions payable to the scheme for each accounting period. The defined benefit accounting would be used only at the consolidation level. In these circumstances, distributable profits of the individual companies are not hit unless and until additional contributions become payable to fund the deficit.

90.6 As noted earlier, the composition of a defined benefit asset or liability will be affected by contributions. The following example illustrates the double entry and the effect on reserves where a defined benefit asset arises from actuarial gains and from overfunding (tax is ignored).

Example

At the beginning of the year, a scheme has no surplus or deficit, the assets and liabilities each being measured at 400.

The pension cost for the year is as follows:

Current service cost	(70)
Interest cost (7%)	(28)
Expected return on assets (8%)	32
Net finance income	4
Total profit and loss charge	(66

Contributions paid during the year were 80.

At the end of the year, a scheme surplus of 39 is measured. Actuarial gains (net) of 25 arise and are recognised in the STRGL. The double-entry would be as follows.

Dr Profit and loss account (net pension cost)	66	
Cr Defined benefit asset/liability		66
Dr Defined benefit asset/liability	80	
Cr Cash (contributions paid)		80
Dr Defined benefit asset/liability	25	
Cr Pension reserve – STRGL (actuarial gain)		25

The pension asset arises as follows:

	Dr	Cr
Asset b/f	Nil	
Pension cost (profit and loss account)		66
Contributions paid	80	
Actuarial gain (STRGL)	25	
Asset c/f		39

The composition of the pension asset could be analysed as follows:

Amount	Nature of asset	Component of reserves
14	Prepaid contributions	P&L reserve
25	Actuarial gain	Pension reserve

In this analysis, the pension asset of 39 is regarded as comprising two components:

- A 'prepayment' of 14, being the difference between the profit and loss charge (66) and the contributions paid (80). This might be regarded as an investment of profits already made.

- An actuarial gain of 25, which has been credited to reserves (either profit and loss reserve or, as in this example, a separate pension reserve). Since this is in the nature of a revaluation gain, it would be regarded as unrealised.

Whilst this might seem to be the purist answer, in practice tracking the components like this will sometimes be over-complex. The whole of the pension asset (or liability) could be regarded as a component of profit and loss reserves provided that any net asset is regarded as being an unrealised component.

90.7 The next example extends the previous one into the following year. The profit and loss charge is again 66. Contributions are, however, reduced to 50 as a result of the surplus. At the end of the year, a scheme surplus of 15 is measured. The double-entry would be as follows.

Dr Profit and loss account (net pension cost)	66	
Cr Defined benefit asset		66
Dr Defined benefit asset	50	
Cr Cash (contributions paid)		50
Dr Pension reserve – STRGL (actuarial loss)	8	
Cr Defined benefit asset		8

The movements in the pension asset are as follows:

	Dr	Cr
Asset b/f	39	
Pension cost (profit and loss account)		66
Contributions paid	50	
Actuarial loss (STRGL)		8
Asset c/f		15
	89	89

The movements in the components of the reserves relating to the asset could be analysed thus:

	Pension reserve (cumulative actuarial gains)	Profit and loss reserve (prepayment)
B/f	25	14
Reduction in contributions	(2)	(14)
Actuarial loss	(8)	–
C/f	15	–

In this analysis, the pension asset of 15 is now equal to the cumulative actuarial gains (less losses):

■ The difference of 16 between the profit and loss charge (66) and the contributions paid (50) results in a 'claw-back' of the 'prepayment' (14) and the realisation of part of the cumulative actuarial gain (2).

■ The actuarial loss of 8 is debited to the pension reserve and reported in the STRGL. Net cumulative actuarial gains carried forward of 15 would be regarded as unrealised.

Comparative amounts

91 There is a general requirement in companies legislation and accounting standards for comparative figures to be given. It should be noted that this requirement applies to the disclosures specified in paragraphs 78 and 80 relating to the position at the beginning of the period.

91.1 The specific requirement relating to comparatives means that the following disclosures are required for the position at three year ends, that is the current year end, the previous year end and the beginning of the comparative period:

- The main financial assumptions used by the actuary (paragraph 78).

- The expected rate of return on each class of scheme assets (paragraph 80).

- The fair value of each class of scheme assets (paragraph 80).

For the above items, the information relating to the position at the beginning of the comparative period is relevant to understanding the pension costs for that period, since they were based on the assumptions set at the beginning of the period.

Entities with more than one scheme

92   Where an employer has more than one defined benefit scheme, disclosures may be made in total, separately for each scheme, or in such groupings as are considered to be the most useful. When an employer provides disclosures in total for a number of schemes, the assumptions should be given in the form of weighted averages or of relatively narrow ranges with any outside the range disclosed separately.

93   Useful groupings of schemes for disclosure purposes may be based on:

(a) the geographical location of the schemes, for example by distinguishing UK schemes from overseas schemes; or

(b) whether the schemes are subject to significantly different risks, for example pension schemes and retirement medical care schemes.

Date from which effective and transitional arrangements

94   The following amounts, measured in accordance with the requirements of the FRS, should be disclosed in the notes to the financial statements:

(a) for financial statements relating to accounting periods ending on or after 22 June 2001: the disclosures required by paragraphs 76-81 and 88-93 of the FRS relating to the closing balance sheet (without comparatives for the previous period);

(b) in addition, for financial statements relating to accounting periods ending on or after 22 June 2002:

(i)   the disclosures required by paragraphs 76-81 and 88-93 of the FRS relating to the opening balance sheet (without comparatives for the previous period);

(ii)   the disclosures required by paragraphs 82-85 of the FRS relating to the performance statements (without comparatives for the previous period); and

(iii) the disclosures required by paragraph 86 for the current period only.

None of these amounts need be recognised in the primary statements in these financial statements.

94.1 For companies that defer implementation of the FRS, an interim disclosure regime starts from June 2001. In addition, the disclosures required by SSAP 24 continue to apply until FRS 17 is adopted in full. The following example is indicative of the transitional disclosures required by FRS 17 (in addition to the SSAP 24 disclosures) for the first transitional year, that is for years ending from June 2001 to May 2002. The example (assuming a December 2001 year end) is based on the full disclosure example in Appendix 1 of the FRS – no changes have been made to that example other than to exclude the disclosures that are not required in the first transitional year.

Pension cost note – FRS 17 disclosures 31 December 2001

Composition of the schemes

The group operates a defined benefit scheme in the UK. A full actuarial valuation was carried out at 31 December 2001 by a qualified independent actuary. The major assumptions used by the actuary were:

Rate of increase in salaries	5.5%
Rate of increase in pensions in payment	3.0%
Discount rate	7.0%
Inflation assumption	4.0%

The assets in the scheme and the expected rate of return were:

	Long-term rate of return expected at 31.12.01	Value at 31.12.01 £ million
Equities	8.0%	721
Bonds	6.0%	192
Property	6.1%	49
		962

The following amounts at 31 December 2001 were measured in accordance with the requirements of FRS 17.

	£ million
Total market value of assets	962
Present value of scheme liabilities	(758)
Surplus in the scheme	204
Related deferred tax liability	(61)
Net pension asset	143

If the above amounts had been recognised in the financial statements, the group's net assets and profit and loss reserve at 31 December 2001 would be as follows:

	£ million
Net assets excluding pension asset	650
Pension asset	143
Net assets including pension asset	793
Profit and loss reserve excluding pension asset	350
Pension reserve	143
Profit and loss reserve	493

94.2 The following example is indicative of the transitional disclosures required by FRS 17 (in addition to the SSAP 24 disclosures) for the second transitional year, that is for years ending from June 2002 to May 2003, if the FRS has not been implemented in full. In addition, the disclosures required by SSAP 24 continue to apply until FRS 17 is adopted in full. This example (assuming a December 2002 year end) is also based on the full disclosure example in Appendix 1 of the FRS.

Pension cost note – FRS 17 disclosures 31 December 2002

Composition of the schemes

The group operates a defined benefit scheme in the UK. A full actuarial valuation was carried out at 31 December 2001 and updated to 31 December 2002 by a qualified independent actuary. The major assumptions used by the actuary were:

	31.12.02	31.12.01
Rate of increase in salaries	**4.0%**	5.5%
Rate of increase in pensions in payment	**2.0%**	3.0%
Discount rate	**4.5%**	7.0%
Inflation assumption	**2.5%**	4.0%

The assets in the scheme and the expected rate of return were:

	Long-term rate of return expected at 31.12.02	Value at 31.12.02 £ million	Long-term rate of return expected at 31.12.01	Value at 31.12.01 £ million
Equities	7.3%	1,116	8.0%	721
Bonds	5.5%	298	6.0%	192
Property	6.0%	74	6.1%	49
		1,488		962

The following amounts at 31 December 2002 and 31 December 2001 were measured in accordance with the requirements of FRS 17.

	2002 £ million	2001 £ million
Total market value of assets	1,488	962
Present value of scheme liabilities	(1,009)	(758)
Surplus in the scheme	479	204
Related deferred tax liability	(144)	(61)
Net pension asset	335	143

If the above amounts had been recognised in the financial statements, the group's net assets and profit and loss reserve at 31December 2002 and 31 December 2001would be as follows:

	2002 £ million	2001 £ million
Net assets excluding pension asset	700	650
Pension asset	335	143
Net assets including pension asset	1,035	793
Profit and loss reserve excluding pension asset	400	350
Pension reserve	335	143
Profit and loss reserve	735	493

The following amounts would have been recognised in the performance statements in the year to 31 December 2002 under the requirements of FRS 17:

	£ million
Operating profit:	
Current service cost	34
Past service cost	12
Total operating charge	46
Other finance income	
Expected return on pension scheme assets	73
Interest on pension scheme liabilities	(53)
Net return	20
Statement of total recognised gains and losses (STRGL)	
Actual return less expected return on pension scheme assets	480
Experience gains and losses arising on the scheme liabilities	(58)
Changes in assumptions underlying the present value of the scheme liabilities	(146)
Actuarial gain recognised in STRGL	276

Movement in surplus during the year	
Surplus in scheme at beginning of the year	204
Movement in year:	
Current service cost	(34)
Contributions	25
Past service costs	(12)
Other finance income	20
Actuarial gain	276
Surplus in scheme at end of the year	479

The full actuarial valuation at 31 December 2001 showed an increase in the surplus from £92 million to £204 million. Improvements in benefits costing £12 million were made in 2002 and contributions reduced to £25 million (8 per cent of pensionable pay). It has been agreed with the trustees that contributions for the next three years will remain at that level.

Details of experience gains and losses for the year to 31 December 2002

Difference between the expected and actual return on scheme assets:	
Amount (£ million)	480
Percentage of scheme assets	32%
Experience gains and losses on scheme liabilities:	
Amount (£ million)	(58)
Percentage of the present value of the scheme liabilities	(6%)
Total amount recognised in statement of total recognised gains and losses:	
Amount (£ million)	276
Percentage of the present value of the scheme liabilities	27%

95   All the requirements of the FRS should be regarded as standard for accounting periods ending on or after 22 June 2003. Earlier adoption is encouraged.

96   Gains and losses arising on the initial recognition of items in the primary statements under the FRS should be dealt with as prior period adjustments in accordance with FRS 3. It is not required to create retrospectively the five-year history of amounts recognised in the statement of total recognised gains and losses beyond those figures already disclosed in financial statements under paragraph 94 above.

96.1 When the accounting provisions of FRS 17 are adopted, a prior period adjustment is required. Any existing pension balances in the balance sheet (including related deferred tax balances) recognised under SSAP 24 will be replaced with any assets or liabilities measured and recognised in accordance with the FRS. Comparative figures in the profit and loss account and STRGL will be revised accordingly. If advantage is taken of the transitional arrangements, all the required comparatives will be available from the previous years' disclosures when the FRS has to be implemented in full.

97 FRS 7 requires the fair value of the deficit or surplus to be recognised as part of a business acquisition. This FRS applies the same policy in requiring the fair value of the defined benefit asset/liability to be recognised. The method of arriving at fair value under this FRS may be different from that previously used on acquisition, but any such difference should be treated as a change in assumptions (ie an actuarial gain or loss) arising since acquisition. Goodwill arising on the acquisition should not, therefore, be restated.

Acquisition accounting issues

97.1 Arrangements for transferring defined benefit pensions obligations when an acquisition takes place are many, varied and often complex. They may include the acquisition of all schemes in an acquired group or, in the case of a business acquisition, the transfer of assets from the vendor's scheme to the purchaser's scheme reflecting transfer values of the accumulated pension rights of individual employees transferred. The value of the assets of an acquired scheme may differ from the value of the scheme's liabilities at the date of acquisition. In acquisition accounting, the surplus or deficit should generally be recognised as an asset or liability in the fair value exercise.

97.2 FRS 7 does not (before its amendment by FRS 17) prescribe any rules for measuring the amount of surplus or deficit to be recognised. The standard merely explains that the actuarial valuation depends on several assumptions about the future; and the *acquirer* would apply its own judgement in determining these assumptions. [FRS 7 para 73]. Generally, therefore, an actuarial valuation should be carried out as at the date of acquisition using actuarial methods and assumptions that are consistent with those the acquirer normally uses for the purpose of determining pension costs. These may differ from those previously used by the acquired company. Before FRS 17, the valuation methods and assumptions would be consistent with those used for SSAP 24 accounting.

97.3 FRS 17 interacts well with FRS 7. Paragraph 101 of FRS 17 has amended FRS 7 to require that a surplus or deficiency as at the date of acquisition is measured consistently with how the acquirer would measure it under FRS 17. In future, the accounting where an acquisition takes place will be consistent with the normal (pre-acquisition) accounting for such pension schemes, as surpluses and deficiencies will be recognised on the balance sheet. There will no longer be dislocation of the acquired company's pre-acquisition and post-acquisition results as a result of changing from spreading to recognising in full the surplus or deficiency at the date of acquisition.

97.4 Where a surplus is large, FRS 7 may also limit the amount of surplus that should be recognised as an asset in the fair value exercise. Whilst the philosophy behind the limitation was similar to that behind the restriction on the recognition of a surplus in FRS 17, that is the resulting asset is subject to a recoverability test, the amendment to FRS 7 ensures the recognition criteria are in future the same under both standards. For example, under the amended wording, a refund that was being negotiated around the time of an acquisition could not be taken into account in estimating the recoverable surplus, unless the refund had been agreed by the pension scheme trustees at the date of acquisition.

97.5 The FRS does not address the question of how surpluses or deficiencies should be measured on acquisitions made during the transitional period, that is should FRS 17 or SSAP 24 measurement principles be adopted before FRS 17 is implemented in full. SSAP 24 does not deal with acquisitions at all. It could be argued that the overriding principle of fair value in FRS 7 would at least not preclude the fair value of a surplus or deficiency at the date of acquisition from being measured following FRS 17's measurement principles.

97.6   FRS 7 does not permit the valuation of surplus or deficiency at the date of acquisition to take into account the cost of any retrospective changes in benefits and membership that are decided on by the acquirer. Such costs should be reflected in the acquiring group's post-acquisition performance statements. Examples are:

- Costs of benefit improvements following the acquisition (treated as past service costs – charged in the profit and loss account immediately or over the period until the benefits vest).

- Pension effect of a significant reduction in the number of employees following a post-acquisition reorganisation (treated as a gain or loss on curtailment – recognised immediately in the profit and loss account).

- Cost of enhanced pensions initiated by the acquirer to induce early retirement (treated as past service costs – charged immediately in the profit and loss account).

Withdrawal of SSAP 24 and UITF Abstracts 6 and 18 and amendment of other accounting standards

98   When applied in full, the FRS supersedes SSAP 24 'Accounting for pension costs', UITF Abstract 6 'Accounting for post-retirement benefits other than pensions' and UITF Abstract 18 'Pension costs following the 1997 tax changes in respect of dividend income'.

99   SSAP 15 'Accounting for deferred tax' is amended as follows:

   (a) the following sentence should be added to the end of paragraph 16 "An exception to this rule is required by FRS 17 'Retirement Benefits'."

   (b) in paragraph 32A the words "SSAP 24 'Accounting for pension costs' and UITF 6 'Accounting for post-retirement benefits other than pensions'" **are replaced by** "FRS 17 'Retirement Benefits'".

100   In FRS 5 'Reporting the Substance of Transactions', paragraph 44 is amended as follows:

   (a) in the first sentence the words, "SSAP 24 'Accounting for pension costs'" **are replaced by** "FRS 17 'Retirement Benefits'".

   (b) in the second sentence the words "SSAP 24" **are replaced by** "FRS 17".

101   FRS 7 'Fair Values in Acquisition Accounting' is amended as follows:

   (a) in paragraph 19 the words "to the extent that it is reasonably expected to be realised" **are replaced by** "to the extent that it can be recovered through reduced contributions or through refunds from the scheme".

(b) the final sentence of paragraph 70 is deleted.

(c) the text of paragraph 71 is replaced by:

"The fair value of the deficiency or surplus should be measured in accordance with the requirements of FRS 17 'Retirement Benefits'. The extent to which a surplus can be recovered should also be determined in accordance with the requirements of FRS 17."

(d) paragraph 72 is deleted.

(e) in the final sentence of paragraph 73 the words "SSAP 24" are replaced by "FRS 17".

(f) the following footnote is added to the last sentence of paragraph 42 of Appendix III:

"This requirement was amended by FRS 17 so that a surplus is recognised to the extent that it can be recovered through reduced contributions or through refunds from the scheme."

(g) the following footnote is added to the last sentence of paragraph 43 of Appendix III:

"SSAP 24 was superseded by FRS 17."

102 FRS 12 'Provisions, Contingent Liabilities and Contingent Assets' is amended as follows:

(a) in paragraph 8 the words "SSAP 24 'Accounting for pension costs'" are replaced by "FRS 17 'Retirement Benefits'".

(b) in paragraph 48 the words "a financial item adjacent to interest but should be shown separately from other interest either on the face of the profit and loss account or in a note" are replaced by "other finance costs adjacent to interest".

103 In FRS 13 paragraph 5 the words "SSAP 24 'Accounting for pension costs' and UITF Abstract 6 'Accounting for post-retirement benefits other than pensions'" are replaced by "FRS 17 'Retirement Benefits'".

104 In UITF Abstract 4 'Presentation of long-term debtors in current assets' the following footnote is added to the end of the second sentence in paragraph 2:

"Under FRS 17 'Retirement Benefits', the pension asset or liability will be shown separately rather than under these format headings."

105 In UITF Abstract 13 'Accounting for ESOP trusts', Appendix I, third paragraph, the words "SSAP 24" are replaced by "FRS 17 'Retirement Benefits'".

Adoption of FRS 17 by the Board

Financial Reporting Standard 17 'Retirement Benefits' was approved for issue by the ten members of the Accounting Standards Board.

Sir David Tweedie   (Chairman)

Allan Cook CBE   (Technical Director)

David Allvey

Ian Brindle

Dr John Buchanan

John Coombe

Huw Jones

Isobel Sharp

Professor Geoffrey Whittington

Ken Wild

Appendix I

Disclosure example

Balance sheet presentation

	20X2 £ million	20X1 £ million
Net assets excluding pension asset	700	650
Pension asset	335	143
Net assets including pension asset	1,035	793

Reserves note

	20X2 £ million	20X1 £ million
Profit and loss reserve excluding pension asset	400	350
Pension reserve	335	143
Profit and loss reserve	735	493

Pension cost note

Composition of the schemes

The group operates a defined benefit scheme in the UK. A full actuarial valuation was carried out at 31 December 20X1 and updated to 31 December 20X2 by a qualified independent actuary. The major assumptions used by the actuary were:

	At 31/12/X2	At 31/12/X1	At 31/12/X0
Rate of increase in salaries	4.0 %	5.5 %	6.5 %
Rate of increase in pensions in payment	2.0 %	3.0 %	3.5 %
Discount rate	4.5 %	7.0 %	8.5 %
Inflation assumption	2.5 %	4.0 %	5.0 %

The assets in the scheme and the expected rate of return were:

	Long-term rate of return expected at 31/12/X2	Value at 31/12/X2 £ million	Long-term rate of return expected at 31/12/X1	Value at 31/12/X1 £ million	Long-term rate of return expected at 31/12/X0	Value at 31/12/X0 £ million
Equities	7.3%	1,116	8.0%	721	9.3%	570
Bonds	5.5%	298	6.0%	192	8.0%	152
Property	6.0%	74	6.1%	49	7.9%	38
Total market value of assets		**1,488**		**962**		**760**
Present value of scheme liabilities		**(1,009)**		**(758)**		**(668)**
Surplus in the scheme		**479**		**204**		**92**
Related deferred tax liability		**(144)**		**(61)**		**(28)**
Net pension asset		**335**		**143**		**64**

[Note: shaded figures not mandatory under the FRS]

Analysis of the amount charged to operating profit

	20X2 £ million	20X1 £ million
Current service cost	34	25
Past service cost	12	–
Total operating charge	46	25

Analysis of the amount credited to other finance income

	20X2 £ million	20X1 £ million
Expected return on pension scheme assets	73	68
Interest on pension scheme liabilities	(53)	(57)
Net return	20	11

Analysis of amount recognised in statement of total recognised gains and losses (STRGL)

	20X2 £ million	20X1 £ million
Actual return less expected return on pension scheme assets	480	138
Experience gains and losses arising on the scheme liabilities	(58)	(6)
Changes in assumptions underlying the present value of the scheme liabilities	(146)	(41)
Actuarial gain recognised in STRGL	276	91

Movement in surplus during the year

	20X2 £ million	20X1 £ million
Surplus in scheme at beginning of the year	204	92
Movement in year:		
Current service cost	(34)	(25)
Contributions	25	35
Past service costs	(12)	–
Other finance income	20	11
Actuarial gain	<u>276</u>	<u>91</u>
Surplus in scheme at end of the year	<u>479</u>	<u>204</u>

The full actuarial valuation at 31 December 20X1 showed an increase in the surplus from £92 million to £204 million. Improvements in benefits costing £12 million were made in 20X2 and contributions reduced to £25 million (8 per cent of pensionable pay). It has been agreed with the trustees that contributions for the next three years will remain at that level.

History of experience gains and losses

	20X2	20X1	20X0	20W9	20W8
Difference between the expected and actual return on scheme assets:					
amount (£ million)	480	138	(6)	94	(73)
percentage of scheme assets	32%	14%	(1%)	16%	(26%)
Experience gains and losses on scheme liabilities:					
amount (£ million)	(58)	(6)	34	25	(23)
percentage of the present value of the scheme liabilities	(6%)	(1%)	5%	2%	(2%)
Total amount recognised in statement of total recognised gains and losses:					
amount (£ million)	276	91	1	66	(158)
percentage of the present value of the scheme liabilities	27%	12%	0%	5%	(14%)

Appendix II

Note on legal requirements

Great Britain

1   The statutory requirements relating to the presentation of pension costs in company accounts are set out in the Companies Act 1985. The relevant requirements are contained in Schedule 4 and are summarised below. Schedule 4 to the Act does not apply to banking and insurance companies and groups, nor to small companies to the extent that they choose instead to comply with the reduced requirements set out in Schedule 8. Requirements corresponding to those of Schedule 4 are set out for banking companies and groups in Schedule 9 and for insurance companies and groups in Schedule 9A.

2   The specific references in Schedule 4 include the following:

(a) the balance sheet formats include a heading:

   "Provisions for liabilities and charges:

   1   Pensions and similar obligations".

(b) the profit and loss formats 2 and 4 include a heading:

   "Staff costs:

   (a) wages and salaries

   (b) social security costs

   (c) other pension costs".

(c) When profit and loss formats 1 and 3 are used, paragraph 56(4) requires the information in (b) to be disclosed.

3   Pension costs are defined in paragraph 94 of Schedule 4 as follows:

> '"Pension costs" includes any costs incurred by the company in respect of any pension scheme established for the purpose of providing pensions for persons currently or formerly employed by the company, any sums set aside for the future payment of pensions directly by the company to current or former employees and any pensions paid directly to such persons without having first been set aside.'

4   Paragraph 50(4) requires disclosure of particulars of any pension commitments under any provision shown in the company's balance sheet and any such commitments for which no provision has been made.

5   The requirements in the FRS regarding the recognition of the amounts arising from a defined benefit scheme are that:

(a) the service cost should be presented within operating profit in the profit and loss account;

(b) the interest cost and expected return on assets should be presented as a net financial item in the profit and loss account;

(c) actuarial gains and losses should be recognised in the statement of total recognised gains and losses; and

(d) the net pension asset or liability should be presented separately on the face of the balance sheet following other net assets and before capital and reserves.

6   The Board has received legal advice that these requirements do not contravene the Companies Act 1985 but that the interest cost and expected return should be presented in a new format heading separate from "interest and similar charges". Accordingly the FRS requires these items to be included as other finance costs (or income) adjacent to interest.

Northern Ireland and the Republic of Ireland

7   The relevant references to companies legislation in Northern Ireland and the Republic of Ireland are as follows:

Great Britain	Northern Ireland	Republic of Ireland
Companies Act 1985: Schedule 4:	Companies (Northern Ireland) Order 1986: Schedule 4:	The Schedule to the Companies (Amendment) Act 1986:
paragraph 8	paragraph 8	paragraph 3
paragraph 50(4)	paragraph 50(4)	paragraph 36(4)
paragraph 56(4)	paragraph 56(4)	paragraph 42(2)
paragraph 94	paragraph 92	paragraph 74*
Schedule 8	Schedule 8	no equivalent
Schedule 9	Schedule 9	European Communities (Credit Institutions: Accounts) Regulations 1992
Schedule 9A	Schedule 9A	European Communities (Insurance Undertakings: Accounts) Regulations 1996

* *Note* The definition of pension costs in the Republic of Ireland legislation is slightly different from that in UK legislation (see paragraph 3) and is as follows:

> '…"pension costs" include any other contributions by a company for the purposes of any pension scheme established for the purpose of providing pensions for persons employed by the company, any sum set aside for that purpose and any amounts paid by the company in respect of pensions without first being so set aside'

Appendix III

Compliance with International Accounting Standards

1   The requirements for retirement benefit costs are included in International Accounting Standard (IAS) 19 (revised 1998) 'Employee Benefits'. The requirements of the FRS are consistent with IAS 19 (revised) in most respects. The only major difference is the recognition of actuarial gains and losses.

2   The FRS requires actuarial gains and losses to be recognised, immediately they occur, in the statement of total recognised gains and losses. IAS 19 (revised) requires actuarial gains and losses to be recognised in the profit and loss account to the extent that they exceed 10 per cent of the greater of the gross assets or gross liabilities in the scheme.[*] Recognition of actuarial gains and losses exceeding the 10 per cent corridor may be spread forward over the expected average remaining working lives of the employees participating in the scheme.

3   The structure for reporting financial performance is more developed in the UK and the Republic of Ireland than under IASs: a second performance statement – the statement of total recognised gains and losses – was introduced by FRS 3 'Reporting Financial Performance' in 1992, whereas no such statement is used in practice under IASs. For the reasons set out in Appendix IV paragraphs 34-47, the Board believes that immediate recognition in the statement of total recognised gains and losses is a major improvement from the traditional treatment of spreading actuarial gains and losses forward in the profit and loss account.

---

[*] *Recognition of actuarial gains and losses within the 10 per cent corridor is allowed but not required*

4   There is some indication that the International Accounting Standards Committee (IASC) may also wish to follow this route once it has moved forward with its work on reporting financial performance.* In IAS 19 (revised), Appendix 3 'Basis for Conclusions' discusses the option of immediate recognition of actuarial gains and losses in a second performance statement. It states that:

> "the [IASC] Board found the immediate recognition approach attractive. However, the [IASC] Board believes that it is not feasible to use this approach for actuarial gains and losses until the [IASC] Board resolves substantial issues about performance reporting. When the [IASC] Board makes further progress with those issues, it may decide to revisit the treatment of actuarial gains and losses."

---

* *IASC is currently (November 2000) working on a project on reporting financial performance.*

Appendix IV

The development of the FRS

Background to the FRS

1   The FRS has been developed from the proposals set out in FRED 20 'Retirement Benefits', which was published in November 1999. FRED 20 was itself the result of many years' deliberations by the Board in which a number of factors were influential, in particular:

(a) concerns in the UK about the existing standard, SSAP 24 'Accounting for pension costs';

(b) the trend internationally towards the use of fair values for pension cost accounting; and

(c) the move within the UK actuarial profession away from traditional actuarial valuation methodologies to a greater use of market values.

2   The main concerns about SSAP 24 were:

(a) there were too many options available to the preparers of accounts, leading to inconsistency in accounting practice and allowing a great deal of flexibility to adjust results on a short-term basis; and

(b) the disclosure requirements did not necessarily ensure that the pension cost and related amounts in the balance sheet were adequately explained.

3   In response to these concerns, in June 1995 the Board published a Discussion Paper 'Pension Costs in the Employer's Financial

Statements' which set out two contrasting approaches to accounting for pension costs:

(a) an actuarial approach, which relied on actuarial measurement of pension scheme assets but removed many of the options in SSAP 24 and enhanced the disclosure requirements; and

(b) a market value approach, which was based on measuring the pension scheme assets at market value.

4   The Discussion Paper noted that the Board's initial view was that the actuarial approach was preferable. The market value approach was included because the Board was aware that the International Accounting Standards Committee (IASC) was likely to propose such an approach and the Board wished to gauge UK reaction to it.

5   IASC published an exposure draft, E54, in October 1996 and a revised standard was issued in February 1998. As expected, IAS 19 (revised 1998) 'Employee Benefits' adopts a market value approach that is very similar to the US standard, FAS 87.

6   The Board set out its views on IAS 19 (revised) in a Discussion Paper 'Aspects of Accounting for Pension Costs', published in July 1998. It explained that the Board did not believe that there were sufficient reasons to stand out against the global trend to a market value approach as long as such an approach could be developed in a way that did not introduce undue volatility into the profit and loss account. It was clear that a pensions standard based on actuarial values for assets would be regarded internationally as weak and would not be an approach that other standard-setters would follow. Given this, and the increasing use of market values by the actuarial profession, it concluded that the UK and the Republic of Ireland should move into line with international practice and use market values rather than actuarial values for

scheme assets. This view was accepted by a majority of the respondents to the Discussion Paper.

7   The Discussion Paper then set out some options for how the Board might proceed in developing a standard based on market values. FRED 20 took forward some of those options, and they are now embodied in the FRS, as explained below. The resulting main changes from SSAP 24 are:

(a) measuring pension scheme assets: a move from using an actuarial basis to using market values (this is consistent with IAS 19 (revised) and FAS 87[*]).

(b) the discount rate for scheme liabilities: a move from using the expected rate of return on the scheme assets to a rate that reflects the characteristics of the liabilities (resulting in the use of a high quality corporate bond rate, again consistently with IAS 19 (revised) and FAS 87).

(c) recognition of actuarial gains and losses: a move from gradual recognition of such gains and losses in the profit and loss account to immediate recognition in the statement of total recognised gains and losses (an approach that IAS 19 (revised) indicated a willingness to revisit once further developments have taken place in the IASC project on reporting financial performance (see Appendix III) and which the G4+1 has also supported in general terms[**]).

---

[*] *However, FAS 87 allows the market values to be averaged over a period of up to five years, which the FRS and IAS 19 (revised) do not.*

[**] *The G4+1 is a group of representatives of the national standard-setters of Australia, Canada, New Zealand, the UK and the USA, and of IASC. In the communiqué issued by the G4+1 after its meeting in April 2000, the Group expressed support for the direction of the conclusions in FRED 20.*

(d) as a consequence of (c), the balance sheet shows a pension liability or asset equal to the deficit or recoverable surplus in the scheme.

8   The Board believes that these changes, as well as moving practice in the UK and the Republic of Ireland more into line with international practice, reflect the underlying economics of providing defined benefit promises. The detailed reasoning behind the changes is set out below.

9   In practical terms, the Board believes that the FRS will, when implemented, make the reported amounts for retirement benefits more transparent and easier to understand. The pension scheme assets and liabilities will be measured at fair value. The balance sheet will show the surplus/deficit in the scheme to the extent that the employer expects to benefit/suffer from it. The profit and loss account will show the ongoing service cost, interest cost and expected return on assets while the market fluctuations will be recorded in the statement of total recognised gains and losses.

Measurement of scheme assets and scheme liabilities

Scheme assets

10   As noted above, the Board did not believe that there were sufficient reasons for the UK to differ from the rest of the world by measuring scheme assets at an actuarial value that did not equal fair value. In addition, and perhaps more importantly, it was clear that substantial changes were taking place within the actuarial profession relating to the traditional actuarial methodologies for measuring assets in a pension scheme. Of the actuaries responding to the 1995 Discussion Paper, all but one supported the use of actuarial valuations. Of the actuaries responding to the 1998 Discussion Paper, all but one supported

the use of market values. Given this, and the advantages of market values in terms of objectivity and understandability, the Board believes there is no credible alternative to their use.

Scheme liabilities

11   Ideally, under a market value approach, the scheme liabilities would, like the scheme assets, be measured at market value. However, there is no active market for most defined benefit scheme liabilities. Their fair value has therefore to be estimated using actuarial techniques. There are two families of actuarial methods for valuing defined benefit liabilities: accrued benefits methods and prospective benefits methods. The difference between them lies in their treatment of the time value of money. Under an accrued benefits method each period is allocated its share of the eventual undiscounted cost, the liability arising from the costs to date is discounted and the discount unwinds in the normal manner over the employee's service life. This results in a higher cost at the end of an employee's service life than at the beginning because the effect of discounting the cost lessens as the employee approaches retirement. Under a prospective benefits method, the total cost including all the interest that will accrue is spread evenly over the employee's service life. This does not represent the economic reality that, because of the time value of money, the cost of providing a defined benefit increases nearer retirement and such valuation methods do not, therefore, approximate the fair value of the liability. For this reason, the FRS requires the use of an accrued benefits method.

12   The FRS requires the defined benefit liability to be the best estimate of the present value of the amount that will actually be paid out. For this to be the case, all expected changes in factors affecting the payments should be taken into account. For final salary liabilities, the liability will therefore be based on the expected final salary, not the current salary. Some argue that this is not consistent with FRS 12 'Provisions, Contingent Liabilities

and Contingent Assets' because the employer has some control over the future increases in salary and hence does not have a present obligation relating to those increases. However, there is a difference between a present commitment to pay a pension based on present salary and a present commitment to pay a pension based on final salary, which the Board believes should be reflected in the measurement of the liabilities. The use of expected final salaries is also consistent with IAS 19 (revised) and FAS 87. For retirement healthcare liabilities, calculating the best estimate of the payments to be made in the future means taking into account expected changes in the cost of medical care.

The discount rate

13   In the UK, actuaries have traditionally discounted the liabilities in a defined benefit scheme at the expected rate of return on the assets in the scheme (prudently estimated). IAS 19 (revised) and FAS 87 require the use of a high quality corporate bond rate.

14   The Board believes that the discount rate should reflect the time value of money and the risk associated with the liability. The view put forward in the Discussion Paper published in 1998 was that such a rate could be determined by looking at the rate of return on matching assets. (If the assets exactly matched the liability they must have the same fair value and hence the discount rate appropriate for the liability must be the same as the rate of return on the asset.) Matching assets were expected to be:

(a) for pensions fixed in monetary terms, fixed rate government bonds;

(b) for index-linked pensions in payment and deferred pensions, index-linked government bonds;

(c) for final salary liabilities, a portfolio containing some element of equity investments.

15   However, later research conducted by the Faculty and Institute of
      Actuaries demonstrated from past data that the correlation
      between equities and salaries had not been close and that the best
      match for final salary liabilities was probably index-linked bonds.

16   Some argue that even if there is no close correlation between
      equity and salary growth, it is appropriate to use the expected
      return on equities as the discount rate if the scheme is invested
      therein because, over the long term, that return is relatively
      secure. However, the higher return expected on equities is a
      reward for the risk involved in equity investment. Unless the risk
      matches that associated with the liabilities, discounting the
      liabilities at the higher return anticipates the expected benefit of
      equity investment without recognising the risks involved. The
      higher return should instead be recognised as it is earned over the
      period the equities are held.

17   On the other hand, although index-linked bonds seem to have
      been a better match for final salary liabilities, they are not a
      perfect match and an index-linked bond discount rate would
      ignore some important aspects of a final salary pension liability,
      for example the uncertainty of the amounts ultimately to be paid
      out. The Board has therefore decided not to try to find matching
      assets but to build up the discount rate from its components. As
      noted above, it believes that, if possible, the discount rate should
      reflect:

      (a) the time value of money (given by the rate of return on an
           investment regarded as being risk-free); and

      (b) the risks associated with the liability because of the
           uncertainty surrounding the ultimate cash payments due.

18   The FRS requires the assumptions to reflect the best estimate of
      the ultimate cash flows. The resulting liability is clearly subject
      to uncertainty – the ultimate cash flows are not contractually fixed

and will depend on final salaries, length of retirement etc. The uncertainty of the future cash outflows might be expected to make the liability more onerous – most entities are risk-averse and would prefer to avoid the possibility that the cash flows might be more than expected.

19   However, in many defined benefit schemes, the employer has the option of preventing the cash flows being greater than expected and even of reducing the cash flows if necessary (eg if investment performance has been consistently poor for a long period). These options exist because the best estimate of the cash flows will include expected benefit increases likely to be granted by the employer such as (i) increases in pensions in payment and deferred pensions at above the minimum required by statute or the scheme rules and (ii) increases in benefits arising from salary increases for active members over and above the rate applicable if they left service (it is assumed that an employer would, over any substantial period, have to increase salaries by at least the indexing rate applied to deferred pensions). Although the employer expects to give these increases, they are not guaranteed. If necessary the employer could, in many cases, give lower than expected increases in benefits and give lower than expected salary increases. In extremis, the employer could even close the scheme down.

20   These options are a crucial factor in the operation of UK defined benefit schemes and the level of benefits that is given. Employers' willingness to provide the expected benefits is often based, at least partly, on the assumption that the liability can be funded in equities. The expectation is that a higher return on equities compared with that on less risky investments will make such promises affordable. The employer can bear the risk associated with the higher return because, if equities were to underperform for a long period, the options described above allow the employer to take action to mitigate the financial impact.

21   These options make the liability less onerous and can be reflected by using a discount rate higher than a risk-free rate. In principle, the premium over the risk-free rate should vary from scheme to scheme (and within schemes), reflecting the differing levels of discretion that exist for different scheme liabilities. However, assessing the appropriate premium is difficult and subjective. In the interests of objectivity and international harmonisation, the Board has therefore decided to adopt a standard discount rate: the rate of return on a high quality corporate bond, ie one rated at the level of AA or equivalent status. This includes a small premium above the risk-free rate, which can be regarded as reflecting the options open to the employer to limit the pension scheme liabilities.

22   Reflecting these options in the discount rate is not inconsistent with the proposal in paragraph 31 of the FRS that it is not appropriate to assume a reduction in benefits below those currently promised. It is not appropriate to assume that a curtailment of the scheme will take place in the future but it is appropriate to reflect the value of the *option* to make that curtailment.

Frequency of valuations

23   The FRS requires the actuarial valuation to be updated at each balance sheet date to reflect current conditions. The Board does not believe that this imposes an excessively onerous or impracticable burden on preparers of accounts for two reasons.

(a)   The figures in the profit and loss account are based on assumptions at the beginning of the period, and will therefore be known before the balance sheet date. It is only the figures in the statement of total recognised gains and losses and the balance sheet that depend on the valuation updated at the balance sheet date.

(b) Unless there have been major changes to the scheme, only the financial assumptions and the fair value of the assets need to be updated at the balance sheet date. The actuarial profession is preparing guidance on what the annual update should involve.

Recognition in the balance sheet

24   Pension schemes will not usually be subsidiary (or quasi-subsidiary) undertakings of the employer because defined benefit schemes are controlled by the trustees, not the employer. It is not, therefore, appropriate to consolidate the scheme into the employer's financial statements. A pension scheme can give rise to assets and liabilities of the employer but these are not the gross amounts of the pension scheme assets and liabilities – the employer does not control the assets nor is it directly liable for the pension payments. Instead, the employer has a pension asset or liability to the extent that it is entitled to benefit from any surplus or has a legal or constructive obligation to make good any deficit.

25   Pension schemes differ in this respect from employee share ownership plans (ESOPs). The key difference lies in the control that the employer has over the trust. ESOP trusts are such that the actions that the trustees can take are very limited – the ESOP exists only to hold the sponsoring company's own shares for future distribution to employees. ESOP trusts are designed to ensure that there is minimal risk in practice that the trustees would act other than in accordance with the sponsoring company's wishes. The sponsoring company has, in effect, de facto control. In contrast, for a pension scheme, the trustees' rights and duties are much wider. The employer cannot in practice ensure that the trustees will act as it would wish in many significant areas and, hence, does not control the assets and liabilities in the scheme.

26   Many respondents to FRED 20 questioned whether a surplus in the pension scheme should give rise to any asset in the balance sheet of the employer. Their view was that the employer did not own or control the surplus in the scheme and, hence, it was not appropriate to recognise an asset. The Board's view is that the employer has an asset if it has the right to reduce its contributions in the future. It is unlikely that an employer could be required to make contributions to a scheme in order to maintain a surplus. Accordingly, in general, a surplus will give rise to an asset for the employer.

27   The amount recognised as an asset cannot, of course, exceed the amount that the employer can recover and such a limit is included in the FRS. The limit reflects the maximum that can be recovered through reduced contributions together with any refunds that have been agreed at the balance sheet date. Some argue that the reductions in contributions must be assessed in relation to the funding assumptions rather than the accounting assumptions because it is in relation to funding assumptions alone that the trustees of the scheme will agree to any such reductions. It is true that the trustees will set the contributions based on the funding assumptions, but over the life of the scheme the accounting and funding assumptions must come together. The delay in accessing the surplus does not affect its measurement because, in the period where the company is still making contributions based on funding assumptions, the accounting surplus will be growing because of the return earned by the excess assets in the scheme with the result that the surplus that the employer will eventually recover through reduced contributions in future will be larger. In present value terms (which is how the surplus is measured), the amount by which the employer can benefit is the same.

28   Furthermore, the assumptions required by the FRS are a best estimate. Funding assumptions may well build in an element of prudence. It is not appropriate to reflect an arbitrary element of

prudence in the measurement of the pension asset for financial reporting purposes.

Recognition in the performance statements

Analysis of pension cost

29   The FRS requires the ongoing defined benefit cost to be analysed into (i) the service cost (ii) the interest cost and (iii) the expected return on assets, with (ii) and (iii) presented as finance costs (or income). The Board believes that including the interest cost and the expected return on assets with the service cost within operating activities distorts the operating cost that is shown. For example, the pension cost recorded for an unfunded scheme would be higher than that recorded for a funded scheme with exactly the same pension obligations. This does not properly reflect the fact that the *pension* in both cases costs the same, it is only the funding policy that is different. The interest cost and expected return are matters relating to the financing of the pension promise. The Board believes that the three components of the pension cost and their underlying economic nature are well accepted and understood and, hence, should be reflected in their presentation in the profit and loss account.

Expected return on assets

30   Although the Board wishes to move to market values for retirement benefit accounting, it does not believe that it would be appropriate for the short-term volatility associated with equity returns to be reflected in the profit and loss account. Rather, the profit and loss account should reflect the long-term return that equities are expected to produce with any fluctuations around that return shown in the statement of total recognised gains and losses. The rationale for this view is explained further below (see paragraph 37).

31   In practice, it is difficult to judge the long-term rate of return on equities at any particular date, given that it needs to reflect the current state of the market. The FRS, therefore, requires the disclosure of an analysis of the assets in the scheme and the expected rates of return assumed so that users may assess the assumptions and calculate the effects of making different assumptions. It is to be expected that those using rates at the extremes of the range at any particular date will come under close scrutiny and possible challenge.

32   The higher long-term return expected on equities compensates for the uncertainty over the return. FRED 20 noted that some believe, therefore, that it is not appropriate to recognise the expected higher long-term return in the profit and loss account every year with the fluctuations around the return going to the statement of total recognised gains and losses. Doing so separates the reward for risk (the expected higher return) from the results of taking the risk (the variability in the actual return). It was suggested that an alternative approach would be to record in the profit and loss account a risk-free return on assets (removing the effects of risk to the statement of total recognised gains and losses completely).

33   There was almost no support for this alternative approach in the responses to FRED 20 and it has therefore not been taken forward in the FRS.

Recognition of actuarial gains and losses

34   SSAP 24 required actuarial gains and losses (variations from regular cost) to be recognised gradually over the service lives of the employees. In the 1995 Discussion Paper, under the alternative market value approach, a different treatment was proposed. The profit and loss account would be charged with the cost of pensions earned in the period. Actuarial gains and losses would be recorded in the statement of total recognised gains and losses.

35   This approach was explored in more detail in the 1998 Discussion Paper and in FRED 20. It is based on the view that items of financial performance should be grouped together according to their characteristics. The Board's approach was set out in detail in its Discussion Paper 'Reporting Financial Performance: proposals for change' (June 1999). That Paper explained that, where gains and losses arise predominantly from price changes and relate to assets and liabilities that are held not with a view to benefiting directly from changes in their value but because they are needed for the employer's operating activities (eg a head office), it would be misleading to include those gains and losses within operating profit. Instead, they should be reported as 'other' gains and losses, ie at present within the statement of total recognised gains and losses rather than the profit and loss account.

36   The Board expects to publish shortly a FRED on reporting financial performance. The proposals in the FRED on the reporting of holding gains and losses will be consistent with those in the Discussion Paper noted above.

37   The Board regards actuarial gains and losses as similar in nature to revaluation gains and losses on fixed assets. In relation to the assets in the pension scheme, they are held with a view to producing a relatively secure long-term return that will assist in financing the pension cost. The length of the term, coupled with the options available to the employer to restrict the liability in extreme circumstances, mean that much of the fluctuations in market values does not affect the relatively stable cash flows between the employer and its pension scheme. Market fluctuations are incidental to the main purpose of the pension scheme just as the revaluation gains and losses on a fixed asset are incidental to its main operating role. They are therefore best reported within the statement of total recognised gains and losses.

38 On the scheme liabilities side, the effect of both experience gains and losses and changes in actuarial assumptions is to update the liabilities to reflect current conditions consistent with the current market value used to measure the assets. As with fixed assets, where the profit and loss account reflects the current depreciation charge, so for scheme liabilities the profit and loss account reflects the service cost and interest cost of providing the pension promise. Subsequent changes in the value of the liabilities are generally related to financial assumptions and are caused by general changes in economic conditions. These fluctuations of the liabilities to reflect current market conditions are, like the market value fluctuations of the assets, incidental to the main operating business of the employer.

39 In the periods after their recognition in the statement of total recognised gains and losses, actuarial gains and losses do not change in nature to become operating costs. They should not, therefore, be 'recycled' by recognition in the profit and loss account in later years. (An additional, pragmatic, reason for not recycling the gains and losses is that doing so would introduce volatility into the profit and loss account. Actuarial gains and losses arising under a market value approach are such that, even when spread over the remaining service lives of the employees, they would cause significant fluctuations in the total amount charged to the profit and loss account. Further, there would be problems in knowing how to allocate the recycled amount between operating and financial costs.)

40 In addition to the fact that this approach is consistent with its views on reporting financial performance, the Board prefers immediate recognition in the statement of total recognised gains and losses to the spreading approach required under SSAP 24 for the following reasons.

(a) The balance sheet reflects the surplus (to the extent that the employer can benefit from it) or deficit (to the extent that the employer is obliged to fund it) in the scheme based on the latest actuarial valuation. These amounts meet the Board's definitions of assets and liabilities of the employer. In contrast, under SSAP 24, some actuarial gains and losses were not recognised at the balance sheet date. In a market value model, there is no conceptual reason to defer the recognition of these gains and losses. Deferral means that the asset/liability in the balance sheet does not equal the recoverable surplus or the deficit in the scheme. In fact, it was not uncommon under SSAP 24 for a deficit in the scheme to give rise to a supposed asset in the balance sheet which built up as the deficit was funded faster than it was recognised. Such figures do not meet the Board's definition of assets.

(b) The figures in the balance sheet and performance statements are transparent and easy to understand.

(c) The complex and arbitrary rules needed to govern spreading gains and losses forward are not required.

41   The main concerns expressed about this approach in the responses to the FRED were the following.

(a) The figures in the statement of total recognised gains and losses and balance sheet can be large and volatile. They will distort the financial statements of the employer and will not be understood by users of the accounts.

(b) Some gains and losses are never recorded in the profit and loss account. This concern had two aspects:

(i) Some believed that all gains and losses (in particular, all losses) should be recorded in the profit and loss account at some point. Doing so is necessary for the profit and loss account to show the true margins achieved by the employer.

(ii) Others accepted the distinction in principle between actuarial gains and losses and operating costs but were concerned at the possibility of understating the costs that should be reflected in the profit and loss account. Over-optimistic actuarial assumptions could lead to lower service and interest costs in the profit and loss account, while the difference between the assumptions and actual experience would be reflected as a loss in the statement of total recognised gains and losses.

42   In relation to the point (a), the Board believes that users of accounts are sufficiently sophisticated to view the figures in their proper context. It is important to remember that the amounts reported in the statement of total recognised gains and losses *in any one period* have relatively little significance and should not necessarily cause concern. What matters is *the pattern that emerges over a number of years.* For example, if a substantial actuarial loss arises in one year, but then reverses over the next few years, there may well be no impact on future cash flows. If, on the other hand, the loss does not reverse and perhaps even is repeated, then it is more likely that additional contributions to the pension scheme will be required. Repeated gains or losses may also imply that pension costs in the future will be lower or higher as experience causes the actuary to change his assumptions. These trends will be highlighted by the disclosure of a five-year history of actuarial gains and losses.

43   The different context in which the figures in the statement of total recognised gains and losses and balance sheet need to be viewed is also highlighted by their position in the accounts: the actuarial gains and losses are reported in the statement of total recognised gains and losses, not the profit and loss account (or earnings per

share), and the pension asset/liability is presented at the foot of the balance sheet separately from and after all other net assets.

44   It is of note that all the users responding to FRED 20 supported the approach in the FRED.

45   The Board's view on the fact that the approach in the FRS does not report actuarial gains and losses in the profit and loss account at any time (paragraph 41(b)(i)) is that this is entirely in line with the approach to reporting financial performance set out in the Board's Discussion Paper on the subject – some gains and losses have different characteristics from those that arise from the employer's mainstream operating activities and it is therefore appropriate for them to be reported separately. This does not imply that they are unimportant or can be disregarded in assessing the employer's performance. It is simply a reflection of the fact that they are different in nature from operating gains and losses.

46   The Board accepts that the concern about understating the costs in the profit and loss account is valid (paragraph 41(b)(ii)), although as, with experience, more attention than hitherto is paid to gains and losses reported in the statement of total recognised gains and losses, such manipulation will become less effective. In the meantime, the five-year history of actuarial gains and losses will separately highlight experience gains and losses so that users of the accounts are aware when actuarial assumptions are consistently not being met. It would be expected that, although the assumptions would probably not be met in each and every year, the experience gains and losses would over time compensate for each other. A consistent trend of experience losses (or gains) should cause the preparers of accounts and the auditors to re-examine the assumptions.

47   It is worth noting that an approach that spreads the actuarial gains and losses forward in the profit and loss account is equally open to abuse. Although the losses arising from over-optimistic

assumptions are recognised in the profit and loss account, only a small proportion is recognised in any one year. The beneficial effects of the over-optimistic assumptions outweigh that small proportion until the effect has built up over many (typically twelve to fifteen) years. Such a delay in the bad news hitting the accounts is likely to be more of an incentive to manipulate the assumptions than immediate recognition of the losses in the statement of total recognised gains and losses.

Recognition of past service costs

48   Under SSAP 24 past service costs for current employees were spread forward in the profit and loss account and past service costs for former employees were recognised immediately in the profit and loss account to the extent that they were not covered by a surplus in the scheme.

49   The decision to improve benefits or award new benefits in relation to past service increases the scheme liabilities immediately. If an employee left the day after the increased benefits vested (usually at the time of the award), the transfer value would reflect those increased benefits – no further service from the employee would be required to earn them. The Board does not, therefore, believe that there is any reason to defer recognition of the increased liability beyond the date the benefits vest.

50   This leaves the question of how the cost should be recognised in the performance statements. Many of the respondents to the FRED believed that the cost of the improved benefits should be offset against any surplus in the scheme, with only the excess cost being recognised in the profit and loss account. They argued that this properly reflects the fact that such benefit improvements may have been awarded only because there was a surplus in the scheme and therefore no cash cost to the employer.

51   The Board's view is that although there may be no direct cash cost, by using a surplus in this way the employer loses some of the advantages that it could otherwise obtain, for example reduced contributions. Further, by awarding such benefit improvements, it may be able to reduce other aspects of its staff costs. From this perspective, it seems appropriate that the cost of the benefit improvements should be recognised as an employment cost. The manner in which the cost is funded, whether through cash or the use of a surplus that could otherwise have been used to reduce contributions, does not affect that classification. However, sometimes the benefit improvements are funded out of a surplus that the employer could not otherwise benefit from, ie a surplus so large that the employer could not absorb it fully through reduced contributions (or agreed refunds). In these cases, the surplus will not have been recognised in full previously and to the extent that it has been used to fund the past service costs the unrecognised amount should now be offset against the past service cost in the profit and loss account.

52   This treatment of past service costs (including the use of any irrecoverable surplus) is consistent with IAS 19 (revised).

Impact of limit on balance sheet asset

53   The limit on the amount that can be recognised as an asset in the balance sheet may mean that some part of a surplus is not recognised. The effect of the balance sheet limit might be allocated to the various pension components in the performance statements in a number of ways. The allocation required by the FRS is one that preserves the structure of the ongoing items (ie the current service cost, interest cost and expected return on assets) as far as possible but allows one-off costs (eg past service costs) to be offset against the unrecognised surplus.

Disclosures

54   FRED 20 proposed sufficient disclosures for a reader to understand the various elements that constitute the pension cost and the relationship between the actuarial valuation and the amounts recorded in the balance sheet. These disclosures were largely supported by the respondents to the FRED, with the exception of:

(a) a comment on the difference between the expected rate of return on equities and the AA corporate bond rate; and

(b) the five-year history of amounts recognised in the statement of total recognised gains and losses.

55   The first of these disclosures has been dropped, because the two rates are required to be disclosed anyway and any comment was likely to be couched in terms that added little extra information.

56   The second disclosure has been retained because the Board believes that it helps place in context the actuarial gains or losses in any one year and hence plays an important role in the FRS.

Transitional arrangements

57   The FRS allows for a long implementation period, with disclosures building up in the notes to the accounts. The reasons for this are:

(a) to avoid companies having to revisit previous actuarial valuations;

(b) to give the Board a chance to persuade IASC to follow the UK approach on the immediate recognition of actuarial gains and losses; and

(c) to give preparers and users of accounts the opportunity to become accustomed to the figures arising under the FRS before they are recognised in the primary statements.

Impact on distributable profits

58   Appendix III to FRED 20 set out a possible approach to mitigate the impact on distributable profits of a pension deficit measured and recognised in accordance with the FRED. Some respondents to FRED 20 thought this approach was unsatisfactory in a number of respects. In the light of these responses and because a distribution problem is unlikely to arise often,[*] the Board has decided not to proceed with this approach. It believes that it is better for those few companies that are affected to find appropriate solutions with the help of their legal advisers.

Alternative cash-based approach to pension cost accounting

59   Throughout the development of the FRS, a number of respondents to the various consultation documents raised the possibility of a return to a cash-based method of accounting for pension costs. It was suggested that in the UK the Pensions Act 1995, together with the existing tax regime, would impose such constraints on the contributions that an employer made to an approved UK pension scheme that, for such schemes, the contributions made in each period could be regarded as an appropriate measure for the pension cost for that period. The argument was that, because the scheme could be neither substantially overfunded (the tax limit) nor underfunded (the minimum funding requirement (MFR) of the Pensions Act), the contributions each year must be equivalent to

---

[*] *A distribution problem will arise only when individual company accounts show a defined benefit liability so large that it reduces distributable reserves to below that needed to cover any intended distribution. In this context, it should be noted that the FRS allows an exemption in some circumstances from the recognition of a defined benefit liability in the accounts of individual companies that are members of a group defined benefit scheme.*

the increase in the pension obligation that had arisen that year, ie the pension cost. The cost of implementing an accruals-based system, therefore, exceeded the benefits.

60   This argument does not apply to unfunded or overseas schemes, for which an accruals-based method would still need to be prescribed. Also, pension regulation still allows substantial scope for employers and trustees to agree on different and varying contribution schedules.

61   For example, for a typical UK pension scheme, it would not be unusual for a scheme to be regarded as 100 per cent funded when measured using the test for the upper tax limit on funding, but 150 per cent funded using the MFR test. The profile of some schemes may lead to even larger discrepancies than this. A pension scheme funded between the 100 per cent level on the MFR basis and 100 per cent level on the maximum funding basis may be able to justify paying contributions at any level between zero (ie a temporary contribution holiday) and the full regular cost calculated on a conservative basis. With typical regular cost levels being between 10 per cent and 15 per cent of pensionable salaries, the difference between full regular cost and no contributions whatsoever is likely to be material.

62   The Board does not, therefore, believe that a return to a cash-based method would ensure that the proper cost of a pension is measured and recognised as it arises over the service lives of the employees.

Alternative accounting standards

63   Some respondents to the consultation papers have suggested that if overseas pension schemes have been accounted for under a 'recognised' standard (for example, FAS 87), those figures could be included in UK financial statements without restatement. The same suggestion was made for retirement benefits other than

pensions that have been accounted for under FAS 106. The Board does not accept this suggestion. While it may sometimes be possible, using options in standards, to achieve a high degree of convergence between the effect of each, where there are differences the Board's standards must be followed.